BACK ON TRACKmarks

From Hopeless to Dopeless

Matt Peterson

Support Shoutout

To my wife, Megan. Thank you for always supporting me and pushing me to chase after my calling. You have no doubt been my greatest role model on how to make my dreams become a reality. You bring so much joy and laughter to everyone that you know. I would not be me without you.

My children Christian, Myla, Riley and Marley. You have taught me love and patience that I never knew that I could have. It has truly been a blessing to watch you grow.

My parents Paul and Cheryl, who never stopped fighting for me. You two stepped up for me when I could not. Even after the thousands of reasons I gave you to give up on me, still, you did not. Thank you.

To Casey and Charlotte. You are literally the reason that I am alive. Casey's Law not only saved me, but countless others. From the bottom of my heart, thank you for your dedication, hard work and sacrifice.

Finally, to Kyle and his family. You have been the driving force and motivation for this book. BACK ON TRACKmarks is dedicated to you.

There have been hundreds of people who have helped me get to where I am today. Thank you for all of your love and support.

A Lesson Learned

He was my best friend. My brother. For 15 short and adventurous years, we did everything together. I drank alcohol for the first time with him. I smoked pot for the first time with him. I smoked my first cigarette with him. We got arrested together, had our hearts broken together. We got into fights together and with each other. For 15 years, we shared everything, until one day, our acceptable high school antics were no longer enough; we took fun to another level. We took one too many steps toward the edge that eventually led us both straight to Hell, where we would dance with the devil himself. Dear heroin, fuck you!

Kyle and I spent the best and the worst years of our lives together. We were inseparable. I was intimidated by him when we first met. He was older than I was. He had a shaved head, gauged ears and tattoos. Kyle had this rugged, punk rock look to him. Basically, he was the type of person that I always made a point to try to avoid. I, on the other hand, was a skinny, awkward, and confused preacher's kid. Being an only child, I just wanted to fit in, so I did my best to keep my awkwardness at bay. "Just be cool, Matt. Just do what they do, and you'll be fine."

Prior to our first meeting, I only knew three things about him. I knew that he was older than I, that he was dating a girl named

Caitlin, and that he never took any shit from anybody. I feared him, but after nearly a year of trying to avoid him, the night came. The night that would begin our journey together. I was hanging out with my friend Peter on his front stoop, as I did on any other night when a friend of his approached us and said that there was "a gathering" in the woods. I had zero desire to attend, but Peter was all for it. I followed suit against my better judgment. After the quarter of a mile walk to the end of the street and into the woods, I heard some familiar voices, which calmed my nerves. However, Kyle was there, as well. I knew that there was no getting out of this one. I had to grin and bear it. No more avoiding.

There was a funny smell in the air and a bad taste in my mouth. The son of a preacher found himself in the middle of a circle in the woods smoking pot and drinking Miller Light. Two things that no thirteen-year-old should be experiencing. But right then I realized, this was it! I am free! Like magic, the awkwardness was gone. The fear of Kyle was gone. I was cool. I was accepted. I finally found what I had been in search of for the last decade. I didn't even know that I was searching for anything, but here it was. I had found it! At last, Matthew Peterson had been born at the age of thirteen.

From that night, Kyle and I became closer. The partying continued and increased. The circle that met in the woods every once in a while became an every weekend event. The alcohol was flowing more freely. The pot was being passed around in abundance. Pills even found their way into the circle from time to time. We were the kings and queens of our neighborhood, and nothing could stop us. Nothing else mattered. We were a family. But our family would slowly be replaced by chemicals.

There were eleven of us in the beginning. Peter, the "dirty Mexican" and good friend of mine. Vickie, Tristen, and Caitlin, who would often keep the boys in check, but could also party just as hard as the rest of us. Jordan was the pothead of the bunch. If anyone wanted to smoke, he was the one to call. Oddly, he was a genius. Brothers Josh and Joe and Joe's girlfriend and eventual wife, Lauren. Adam, who would one day be my best man in my wedding, and Kyle.

As more and more drugs and alcohol found their way into our original circle of friends, bonds began to break. Most of the others knew that school and employment needed to be taken more seriously. After just a couple of years, there were now only four. The strong ones. The coolest of the cool. The ones that could "hang." Getting high and drunk was a sport for us. We were always trying to out drink, out smoke, out pop, and out snort each other, and what a sport it was! It was a sport that we began to practice on a daily basis.

For years, Peter, Adam, Kyle, and I would do everything together. We were from the same neighborhood, we went to the same school, carpooled together, we even worked together. If one of us had a problem, we all did. If one of us had money, it was shared with the group. If one of us got into a fight, then we all fought. The four of us were brothers, and nothing could tear us apart. We were ready for anything, and we were proud. However, we had no idea that drugs, the very thing that brought us together, was the very thing, the *only* thing that would destroy us.

Just a few years into our recreational drug-using careers, Kyle and I crossed a line. Without even realizing it, neither one of us were getting high for fun anymore. Our drug use had a special grip on us that was different from the others. It became a need for us to get high to feel right. To feel normal. Just like food, water, and shelter, we had to have it. There was no longer a choice for us to use or not. Kyle and I slowly began to distance ourselves from Peter and Adam. It started with Kyle and me making secret trips to the bathroom so that we could use cocaine or pills without Peter or Adam knowing about it. Looking back on it, I am sure that both of them knew exactly what was going on. Just a few secret trips to the bathroom later, we just stopped hanging out with Peter and Adam altogether.

Then there were two. The last of the original circle. The woods were gone. The friends were gone. The fun was over. What started out as a social gathering that we did for enjoyment, we were now doing alone and in secret. The quality and quantity had increased to the point where we were spending every penny that we had on pills and cocaine just to feel normal. To simply function. To get out of bed or to eat. To interact with another person in any "normal" way. We found ourselves needing the pills to live.

Before we knew it, we had completely replaced each other. Both too proud to admit what was happening to our friendship, our brotherhood. We knew that something was wrong, but, looking back, I don't think either of us really knew what was causing the disconnection. Eventually, we were forced to choose pills over our friendship. For months, we struggled separately and desperately, trying to find ways to get money to support our pill habit, but it was too expensive to continue alone. So, we formed a partnership. Not a friendship. A partnership. Gone were the days of brotherhood, now it was business. We needed one another to get our fix. Every day, we would lie and steal to get just enough to get us through to the next day, where we would do it all over again. Until one day, Kyle broke. Something we had both promised to never do, he did.

Heroin is much less expensive and much more powerful than any pill that we were able to get our hands on. Kyle's choice to move on to heroin forced us to part ways once again. I promised myself that I would never lower myself to that level. Heroin was dirty. I refused to be a junkie. Pills were clean, and, at that time, much more accepted by society thanks to the trigger happy, over-prescribing doctors...

Inevitably, I followed suit. I ended up making the smart and mature choice and began my career as a heroin addict (this is how I

7

justified it to myself). Over time, Kyle and I got back in touch with each other. Neither one of us ever spoke to each other about using heroin. We hid our use from each other. Pride is a bitch sometimes, so we would play it off like we both had our lives in order. We were the fakest best friends in existence. Every once in a while, we would throw hints out to each other that we should go get some heroin, but we would always mask it as a joke to see if one of us would take the bait. After just a couple of months, the day came when we were both sick from going through withdrawal and completely broke. This would begin our partnership once more.

Just like with pills, we needed each other. What was once the cheaper and more powerful choice was now just as expensive as the pills were. Our tolerance for the opiate was through the roof. "Luckily" for us, there was one more level, a next step that we had not yet taken our addiction. Straight to the veins. The final level. We were now living to get high and getting high to live. This would ultimately split us up once again. No more partnership. Heroin and the needle had completely taken over both of our lives, and we would never again get high together.

More than a year had gone by. Surely this could not last forever? Every day was the same. The moment my eyes opened in the morning, the wheels in my head immediately began to turn. What crime do I need to commit today in order to get money? That would range anywhere from panhandling, to manipulating and lying to everyone that I knew, to stealing clothes or electronics from stores that I could either sell for cash or trade to the dope boy. Then came the always exciting trip to Cincinnati to cop some dope. The entire ride, just praying that the police did not pull up behind me and run my plates. Then, back to Kentucky, where it was safe. At least it felt safe...er. Sometimes I could not even wait to get back to the Bluegrass State. I would simply be too sick. So, in that case, I would shoot up while I was driving on the interstate. Then, after all of that was over, I would attempt to get some sleep so I could wake up and do it all over again.

I was either going to die or get arrested. I often wished for death, however, because I knew what I would have to go through if I ever got arrested. Detoxification. Withdrawal, which felt like the flu times 10. The shame of everything that I had done to my family, my friends, and myself to feed my drug habit. I would beg God and the Devil both to come take me, but neither of them would. Instead, they showed up in the form of a Boone County police officer. My parents had issued Casey's Law on me, which meant that I was court-ordered to go to rehab. For exactly one month, I would sit and wait in jail. Waiting for anything to happen.

On a Monday morning, a guard came to get me from my cold, dark cell. Finally, a little bit of freedom. I had exactly two hours to get from the jail to the Grateful Life Center, a long-term men's inpatient facility. I was scared to death, but I was not sure why. I had been offered help. I was given a second chance at life, so why did I want to run and get high instead? The look on my family's face when they saw me walking out of the jail was enough to make me go. Without even saying a word, the look of relief, exhaustion, love, and disgust convinced me to go to rehab.

Before I could even process what was going on and what I was going to be going through, I was sitting in the lobby of the Grateful Life Center ("GLC"). A guy by the name of Jacob was the peer mentor who oversaw taking me through the intake process. It was an emotional few moments for my family and me, but the time quickly came, and we said our goodbyes. I was now a client of a men's inpatient facility. I was in a house with 118 other men who were all going through the same thing as me, but I felt completely alone. Suddenly, I heard something. A voice. I glanced up and see a shaved head, gauged ears, and tattoos. A guy with a tough, rugged, and punk rock look to him. The type of guy that I made a point to avoid. There stood Kyle. The relief that I felt at that moment was almost overwhelming. This, in my opinion, was a God moment. I am not sure if I was more relieved that he was there for his sake or my own, but it did not really matter. We were both there, alive and together again. The feeling of loneliness and fear turned into excitement to see how this next chapter of our lives would play out.

Apparently, he already knew that I was going to be coming into treatment. My name had been up on the "New Client" board for a few days before I had gotten there. As soon as I completed my intake, he immediately walked up to me and gave me a hug. It was the kind of hug that was physically uncomfortable but emotionally soothing. Kyle seemed to be just as relieved as I was.

Kyle showed me the ropes over the next few weeks. He had gotten there a couple of months before I did and had the daily routine down. This included chores every morning, deep clean on Saturdays, what time to get up, what time to go to bed, meetings, Big Book study, classes, and mealtimes. He took me under his wing and made sure that I was taken care of. He introduced me to the right guys and made sure that I had everything that I needed. He even pulled some strings to make sure that he was my "phase guy," which meant that he would be the one who would be responsible for getting me to 12-step meetings outside of the GLC. I cannot express the gratitude I had that he was there, for I would have been lost without him. From 8:00 a.m. to 4:00 p.m. every day, I had to go to three classes which were either focused on the Big Book of Alcoholics Anonymous, or a complete bitch fest if we felt like staff were treating us unfairly (rarely the case as we were the ones who were making things difficult on ourselves), and two Alcoholics Anonymous ("A.A.") meetings. Each day was concluded with two more A.A. meetings at 6:00 and 7:30 p.m. I did not even have time to think most of the time, which was probably good for me. I did not realize it at the time, but staying that busy was an intentional aspect of the treatment program. I mean, what else could a newly-sober heroin addict think about other than all those painful years and the horrible, unspeakable things that I had done? But when those thoughts did come to my mind, there was Kyle, ready and willing to talk me through them. He was my rock and my shoulder to cry on. He saved my life.

The program was long, but Kyle made it through and graduated from treatment. After graduation, he waited his mandatory two weeks before he could move out, then he was gone.

Just like that, he disappeared. I stopped seeing him at meetings. We had no contact over the phone, and he did not come back to visit like he said that he would. This is something that we had all seen time and time again throughout our time in treatment, and the reason was always the same. Relapse. I knew deep down that Kyle, too, had relapsed, but I would not allow myself to believe it. It was short-lived, however. It did not take long for the news to get back to me that it was true. I was hurt, scared, and angry. I just did not understand how he could do that. He was given a second chance at life, and he just threw it all away! I had a good group of guys who helped get me through this time.

Shortly after, my time would also come to graduate and leave the GLC. It was an emotional time. I had never gotten sober before. That place was my foundation. The guys there were my rock. It was scary to think about living life outside of those walls and in the real world instead. A lot of guys that I went through the program with had relapsed once they moved out. Would I? I felt confident and had gained a lot of knowledge while I was there, but so did the other clients who left and relapsed. I began to doubt myself, but when I opened up to my friends about my fear of leaving, they all said that if anyone would stay sober after moving out that it would be me.

So, with my confidence up and my head held high, I moved back home with my parents. The adjustment period was very difficult. I had spent the last eleven months either in jail or in rehab. I had never been sober before and had no idea what to do with my time. Then, life happened, as it does, and I was not prepared to handle it. I, too, would relapse.

Just over a year would go by, a year of the same old behaviors, before I would be fortunate enough to be arrested. After being released from jail, I went straight to the GLC to visit some old friends. I remembered that the GLC was my foundation for my sobriety, and I could not think of a better place to go. I was surprised when I walked through the doors, for there was Kyle standing in the lobby. He was a client of the Grateful Life Center again. I thanked God that he was back. We still had not spoken to each other since he relapsed over a year ago. We tried to spend as much time together as we could, but he was busy at the GLC, and I was busy working and living my life. I was 27 years old at this time and had never actually been a productive member of society before. My adult responsibilities soon took over all my time.

Kyle did what he needed to do to graduate from treatment for the final time. This time, however, he learned from his past, and instead of moving back home with his parents, he moved into a sober living home. Although we did not hang out anymore, we kept in contact every once in a while over the phone.

One more time, about one year later, Kyle would end up saving me. The woman that I was living with, the woman that I was planning to marry decided that she was not ready for the type of commitment that I was wanting. My heart was shattered. My world seemed to have stopped. Crushed, hopeless, and with nowhere to go, I called Kyle. He told me that there was a bed open in the sober living home where he was living, and not only that, but I would be his roommate. I swear, God is a beast!

During that time, all I wanted to do was get high or drunk, or both. I was obsessed and could think about nothing else. So badly, I wanted to get as intoxicated as I could get, hunt down her new boyfriend, and beat the brakes off him. These were all rational thoughts in my mind, but Kyle did not allow me to follow through with any of it. I cannot count how many days he took off work just to be with me to make sure that I did not do anything stupid, how many plans he broke just so I would not have to be alone. It was almost like he put his life on hold, for me. I was no doubt grateful for his sacrifices. However, as I look back on it now, I feel that I was being selfish.

It took me a couple of months to pick the pieces of my heart back up and to get back on my feet. The process was long and very difficult, but I do not even want to think about what I would have done if it had not been for Kyle coaching me through it all. He helped me so much more than he knew. But finally, our friendship was the way that we used to be in the past. The difference this time, though, was that we were both free, and we were both sober. We had never really hung out sober before outside of rehab. We had so many good talks, a ton of laughs, a few tears, and a whole lot of fun. We were both genuinely happy, and life was good! For a few months, at least.

Then something happened. Nothing that I directly witnessed, but I sensed it. Walls began to go up, and distance began to separate Kyle and me. The fun slowed down, and the laughs got softer. The only time that we saw each other was late at night right before we went to bed. The signs told me what was going on, but I refused to allow myself to believe it. No way! There is no way that he relapsed again. I began to justify his actions for him, which was one of the worst things that I could have done. But, after only a week or two, it became undeniable. I knew that he had relapsed again, but instead of confronting him about it and offering him help, I got angry and resentful. Sometimes I would shoot him a text message to make sure that he was alright, but that was about it. I loved him and cared about him, but I did nothing to help him.

Then one day, he finally reached out to me and told me what I already knew. He confessed to me that he was asked to sell some prescription pain pills by a guy that he worked with. Instead of selling them, he ended up taking them and was back on heroin within just a couple of days. Kyle begged me for help. He said that he was willing to do anything, including going back to the Grateful Life Center again. He cried. I had never seen him act like this before. He asked over and over for me not to leave his side because of his fear of what he would do if he was left alone. I did not know that he was literally begging for his life. If I had known, I never would have gone to work that night. I told him to just go back to the house until I got home from work, and then we would hang out.

That would be the last time that I saw or spoke to Kyle. My best friend. My brother. I failed to do for him what he had done so many times for me. For the next three days after our last conversation, the ones who loved him the most were looking for him. Nobody knew where he was, nor could we get ahold of him. I grew more and more angry at him for disappearing like his, and in my final voicemail I left him, I said, "Dude, if you have money for drugs, then you have money to pay your rent and pay me back. By the way, next time you are here, you need to go ahead and pack up your shit and find somewhere else to live."

I called Chris, the owner of the sober living house, and told him that Kyle was no longer living in the house, he owed rent, and that I had not heard from him in days. Chris then told me that he saw Kyle's van at Walmart earlier that day, so we both agreed to meet there to see if his van was still there. It was, and so was Kyle.

On September 23, 2015, I found Kyle. He had passed away from a heroin overdose, alone in the back of his van. I could literally feel the world shrink.

The evening was not over yet, however. After the coroner had finished his work and Kyle was moved, I, accompanied by two Ft. Wright police officers, then went to his father and stepmother's house to inform them. It was late, so I had to knock on the windows to get them to wake up. Finally, they woke up and invited us in. I just stood there in silence. I could not get the words out. I just looked at Gary, his father, until he finally had to ask me, "He's not gone, is he?" I responded with "Yeah, bro," and knelt at his father's feet and cried.

I do not know which part was worse. Finding Kyle, dead from a heroin overdose in the back of his van, or the look on his father's face when I had to tell him that I found his son. Those are two images that have been permanently etched into my brain.

If you have a loved one who is struggling with addiction, please keep your eyes, mind, and heart open. They are literally fighting for their life. If your loved one comes to you for help, like Kyle came to me, drop everything and help them! Kyle cried and begged me for help, to not leave his side, but I blew my one and only chance. There is a very small window of opportunity when an addict reaches out for help. Do not miss your chance to save their life. I promise you, that is a regret that you will not want to live with. It was September 23, 2015, when I had to learn this lesson. I have not forgiven myself for it. I still cry about it often. I replay it in my mind over and over again, wondering how it could have been different. Could I have saved him? Am I the reason that he died? What if I did not go to work that night? What if? What if? This is a lesson that I hope you do not have to learn. Kyle taught me this lesson with his life

For Kyle and the entire Ossege Family.

I love you and I am sorry.

A Song for Him

Written by

Adam Weeden, brother and best friend of Kyle and I

It was raining on that day

The air was bitter cold

All your friends came out to see you

All your family, young and old

When I shook your father's hand

Felt pain behind his eyes

When I saw your brother smile

Felt something missing inside

And when we put you in the dirt

I couldn't help but smirk

I guess we'll carry on

I'll figure it out

Guess I'll make the time

To figure it out

My Story

How It All Began

I glance over to my right and I see them. Two headlights, spotlights almost, coming straight at me. I feel the impact followed by my weightless body spinning through the air. It felt like minutes. Moments later, I do not know how long I was unconscious, I open my eyes to find paramedics, police and flashing lights everywhere. I quickly notice that I cannot move my legs, so I do my best to squirm so that I can catch a glimpse of my two friends, Brandon and Sarah. A paramedic nearly jumps on top of me, pinning me to the wet pavement and giving me a strong warning to lie still for my own sake. I still manage to get my eyes on them. Sarah was sitting up, crying. It was more of a scared cry rather than a hurt cry. Brandon, however, was still underneath the van with his head just inches away from the rear tires. In the position that he was laying, the number of paramedics around him and with the way that Sarah was crying, I thought that he was dead. But, just a few seconds later, Brandon began to try to sit up.

The three of us were running across a busy, four-lane highway to get to our church, which is where my mother was. We did not make it, obviously. We began to run across when we realized that there was a church van driving straight for us. Brandon and I got the worst of the accident, so we were strapped onto those fancy surfboards and loaded into the back of an ambulance. While Brandon and I were both hit by the van, Sarah actually ran into the van. The three of us got a lot of good laughs out of that one.

Once we got to the hospital, Brandon had the scrapes on his knees and face taken care of, while I tried to walk. By the grace of God, I was not paralyzed, but my hip was badly bruised. We seemed to have escaped death that night, but I had no idea that that night would bring me even closer to death years later. That night is when my journey began. I was eleven years old.

My upbringing was great. I received good grades in school. I had friends. My parents provided me with everything that I needed and much of what I wanted. My father was a pastor of a Southern Baptist church and loved my mother. He still does. But best of all, I am an only child, and from what I was told, I was a great kid. Minus the fact that I did not sleep through the night until I was three years old. However, after that night when I had the close encounter with a van, my life began to change. I slowly began to lose interest in school and my grades began to fall. My choice of friends changed, and I started to hang out with the crowd that rebelled from their teachers and parents and enjoyed loud music. The good preacher's son began to change.

Within two years from the accident, when I was thirteen years old, I found myself in the crowd of "cool kids" from my neighborhood. School became an inconvenience. It was not fair that

I was being forced to go to a place for seven hours a day when I could be running around and causing mayhem in my neighborhood instead. My parents did not understand; after all, that wasn't how they raised me to behave. But in the summer between eighth grade and my freshman year of high school, the fun really went up a notch. Drugs. Alcohol. Sex. These three things became my driving force, and my good upbringing now meant nothing. Starting off on weekends, a group of us would sneak off into the woods to drink beer, which was stolen from someone's parents, and smoke pot and cigarettes. All of which I did for the first time in the same night. Every week, I would go through the motions in order to make it to the weekend to do it all over again.

The weekends gradually got longer and longer. At first, the fun was had on Friday night and Saturday night. Then Friday, Saturday, and Sunday. Then Thursday. And Wednesday. Until it moved to a daily event. What started off as a social gathering in the woods was now a lifestyle for a couple of us. There were four of us. Pete, Adam, Kyle, and myself, and we separated ourselves from the rest of the group so that we could drink and get high daily without getting judged. The four of us were inseparable. Throughout high school, we rode to school together, fought together, fought each other, got in trouble together, played pool and football together. We did it all.

Kyle and Adam played in a couple of bands together. Kyle was on the drums while Adam played guitar, bass guitar and sang from time to time. They were best friends... most days. Pete also had a passion for music, but never got involved with any of the bands. He and I would normally just smoke pot and watch them practice or watch Family Guy. If not, then we were in Kyle's garage playing pool. Kyle's house was the hangout spot for us. The four of us spent countless hours in his garage smoking, drinking, snorting a buffet of drugs, and playing pool. The four of us were the best of friends; however, if we were not all together, then Kyle and Adam would be doing their thing while Pete and I were doing ours. While Kyle and Adam were more into creative activities like art, poetry, and music, Pete and I were more into sports. We played a lot of frisbee golf and backyard football. Although, there may have been another reason why Pete and I spent more time together. We enjoyed getting high more than they did. Kyle would dabble on occasion with heavier drugs. Adam, on the other hand, never partook in the heavy stuff. Pete and I would do cocaine, Xanax, Percocet, Vicodin, Valium, Morphine, OxyContin, and anything else that we could get our hands on.

Cocaine was my first love. Pete introduced me to it, but with a heavy warning, for he knew how much I enjoyed getting high. He also knew that cocaine could potentially do some real harm to me. I heard his warning but paid no attention to it at all. I was young, invincible, and now in love with cocaine. To put it into perspective, during this time, I was in the "school to work program" at my high school. This meant that I would go to school until 11:00 a.m. I would then go to my first job at a jewelry repair factory from 11:30 a.m. to 5:00 p.m. Then I would go to my second job at a fast-food restaurant from 5:30 to 10:00 p.m. I was a hard worker and managed to save up just over $2,500 in just about one year. All of the money that I had worked so hard for was gone within less than a month after experiencing the incredible effects of cocaine. I was embarrassed and ashamed for spending every penny that I had saved while still in high school, but ironically, the embarrassment and shame were the same things that kept me using. "Well, it's all gone, and I feel like a piece of shit. I might as well just keep using." This is what I told myself. There was another side of me, however, that was saying, "Matt, you are an idiot. Stop now before you lose more than just money!" That side of me just did not seem rational at the time, so I blocked it out.

Although I spent all of my money on cocaine, I never really got addicted to it. I loved the high, but the only time I craved the drug or felt like I needed it was when it was in my system. Especially while I was coming down from the high, which was unbearable. My chest would get tight. My heart would race to the point where I would expect a heart attack to happen at any moment. I would get extremely paranoid, panicky, and I was unable to slow my heart rate started without me. I did not throw a fit about it though; I just continued to my room to change clothes and jump into the party. But before I was even able to finish changing, I heard a knock at the door. It was the police, and my overly polite friends decided to invite them in to participate in the underage drinking and bong hits. Brandon was already asleep, and when the police asked who the pot and alcohol belonged to, nobody said a word. As a result, I was charged with it all. In Kentucky, since nobody fessed up to the illegal shenanigans, I was charged by default since it was my name on the lease. It was my first real consequence from drug and alcohol use. My sentence: three weekends in jail. Not too bad, in my opinion. I was not able to put together, however, that my partying was beginning to become a problem. I had lost thousands of dollars and a few friends because of my cocaine use. Now I have a criminal record from the pot and alcohol. The only thing that I was focused on was that now my back pain was starting to bother me. Or was it? It was not until a few years later that I was informed that substance use can alter the brain's ability to receive and interpret pain signals. This can often increase the feeling of pain, without the pain actually increasing at all. Welcome to the magical world of substance abuse.

  After I had ended my career as a coke head, there always felt like something was missing from my life. At the time, I did not realize it, but I had been craving something subconsciously to fill that hole that was left inside of myself from the cocaine use, for it can take years for the brain to heal itself from heavy drug use. Especially stimulants. The pot and alcohol just were not quenching my thirst like they used to, so to quench the thirst, I began to use pain medication more and more. This seemed to do the trick, for a while, and I had the perfect excuse to use various narcotics, my little run-in with the van years prior. Sometimes I was able to mask my use as a party drug. But in the times that I could not, I could always bring up my past and being hit by that van. I was in pain and all of my friends knew my story. Who could judge me?

The Grip Of Pain Pills

Over time, my pill intake increased. I began to justify my pill use more, which meant that I had to act the part. The more pills that I used, the more that I had to act like my back was hurting. My back pain increased, so my pill intake increased. In reality, my pill intake increased, which made my back pain increase. It is funny what you can see in hindsight. Either way, I took full advantage of the situation. But as this process went on, buying pills from people that I knew no longer made any sense. My tolerance was going up, and the amount of money that I was spending on pain killers was getting fairly expensive. Not only that, but I needed to get into the doctor anyway in order to keep up the act. It was important for me to keep my friends fooled so that they did not think that I had a problem. Honestly, I did not really care what they thought. I just did not feel like dealing with fallout. So, I called my mommy and had her make an appointment for me to see a doctor about my back pain.

This began my career as a "doctor shopper." With the combination of my story about being hit by the church van in seventh grade and my superior acting skills, I was able to get prescriptions from just about every doctor that I had an appointment with. I would go to one doctor for a while until I felt that I needed a higher quality or higher quantity. At that point, my current doctor would then refer me to a different doctor who had the ability to give me what I was searching for. Up the ladder I went. From the emergency room, to my family doctor, to a spine specialist, and all the way up to a pain specialist where I would get more pills and stronger pills each time. Everything was going great until I came across an unexpected problem. The pain specialist was as high as I could go, and he would not increase my dose anymore. At the time, I felt he was being incredibly selfish and unreasonable. After all, as far as he knew, I was in significant, debilitating pain! I needed more, so I had no choice but to take matters into my own hands and begin to buy them off of the street and start combining them with my prescription.

It was not very difficult to see that I had a problem. I was going through 30-day prescriptions in four days and spending hundreds of dollars a week for more pills on top of that. But nobody knew. Everyone close to me thought that I was taking my prescriptions as I was supposed to. Unfortunately for me, I still had that quiet voice in my head saying, "Matt, you really need to get a handle on this."

This time, I actually listened, and once again, I went to my mom so that she could get me into the doctor. Except this time it was not to get pills, it was to get off of them. The only problem was that my parents and I were utterly uneducated about what I was experiencing. None of us were taught anything about addiction or the effects of opiate withdrawal. The only place that we could think of to go was to the emergency room, so that is where I went. From there, I met with a social worker who asked me all kinds of questions about my drug and alcohol use, my home life, my employment, and suicidal thoughts. I answered as honestly as I could. "I am employed. I am a college student. My home life is good. I feel fine. I just need help taking my medication correctly. And of course, I have thought about suicide. You haven't?"

    I really just wanted to know how to take pills successfully, but they did not hesitate to admit me to the psych ward due to my report that I had thought about suicide recently, and I did not hesitate to admit that maybe I overreacted and that going there was a mistake. For the next five days, I experienced real opiate withdrawal for the first time. I was still unaware of what it was at the time. All I knew was that I wanted my pills and that I felt awful. But my pride did not allow me to show any weakness. I spent those five days proving to the nurses and to my parents that this was a mistake and that I was not an addict like they thought. As I said, I was a great actor and manipulator. God and I were the only ones who really knew how I felt.

    On the fifth day, I was released from the hospital to the care of my parents. I told myself that I was going to stay off of the pills since I had been away from them for five days. I was just going to drink and smoke pot like I used to. I made the promise to my parents to no longer take pain medication, and to prove it, I needed to go to the mall to get a new phone and phone number so that my "old friends" could not contact me anymore. My parents agreed and gave me $200 so that I could go get the phone. I did not end up getting the phone that I originally intended to get, however. On that day, they just happened to have a sale going on. All I had to do was pay the tax on a phone and it was mine. So that is was I did. I now had the phone in one pocket and $160 in the other. Now, should I give the rest of the money back to my parents? Or should I just keep it? And if I keep it, what am I going to spend it on? So, I got my pill dealer's phone number out of my old phone before I left the store and called him. It was no more than eight hours since I left the hospital with the promise that I would never use pills again before I was high on Percocet. I picked right back up where I left off.

I did a good job of hiding my use from my family. The hospital called all of my doctors and told them to no longer prescribe my medication to me because I abused it. But my parents did not know that. So, although I had to buy it all off of the streets, my parents thought that I was still taking my prescriptions and also believed that all of my money was going to pay for my doctor visits and prescriptions. It was stressful and expensive, but it was working for a short time. Until I got some news that would put my addiction into overdrive.

35

My grandmother had been in poor health for some time. She had battled cancer and seemed to have been beating it, but eventually, the cancer that started in her kidney was now worse and spreading to her bones. She had been moved to hospice, and one evening we received the phone call informing us that she is being taken off of life support and would be passing at any time. Being the selfish and self-centered drug addict that I was, I used this news as an excuse to use even more. The "pity card" can be a very powerful card to play, and I used it to my advantage. The downside, however, was that my addiction was so far out of control that I used all of my pills before we made the trip to see her. So, with no money and no pills, I rode with my parents on the four-hour trip to Indiana.

My grandmother was one tough lady! She was expected to pass away at any moment, but she held on for four more days, and somehow, I managed to see this as an inconvenience. I was in withdrawal from the first day and each day after that was worse than the last. I was barely hanging on by taking some non-narcotic pain relievers from my aunt, but those were just about useless. On the fourth day, I just could not take it anymore. I had to feel better. My parents drove, so I needed to convince them to let me borrow their car, their debit card and allow me to drive four hours back to Kentucky. I do not remember what story, what lie, I told my parents, but it worked. Just knowing that I was getting closer to getting some pills made me feel better. It was a long and miserable drive, for not only was I in withdrawal, but I also just left my dying grandmother's bedside so that I could go get drugs. But I kept going.

About an hour away from home, I called my dealer to set everything up so that I could get high as soon as I got there. Just like always, my dealer had what I needed, and life was good again. I picked up the drugs, rushed home to the empty house, quickly crushed up the pills into powder and snorted as much as I could fit into my nose. Relief. For a moment anyway. It was not more than a few minutes later that I received a phone call from my mother. "Grandmother passed. It was like she waited for you to leave so that you didn't have to see her go." I lied to my family, left my grandmother, knowing that I would never see her alive again and stole $300 out of my parents' checking account so that I could get high. Then I find out that my grandmother's last act was to die when it was the most convenient for me. The guilt that I felt from everything that had just happened increased my pill use. I felt this new depression, and the only way that I was willing to deal with it was to do as many pills as I could every day. Lying and manipulating the people who still cared about me became a full-time job. Everything became a blur, like I was living in a dream. But one evening, the bad dream would become a nightmare.

The Turning Point

Just as always, I got in touch with my pill guy when I got off of work so that I could get what I needed for the night and part of the next day. This time, though, I got the worst news that any addict could ever get. He was out of pills. The all too familiar feeling of panic hit, but he had an offer for me. He informed me that he did not know where to get any pills, but that he could get me something better. Heroin. Although it was tempting because I knew that I needed to get something in my system before I went into withdrawal, I declined. I did not know much about heroin at the time other than I knew that I should never do it and that it was much more powerful and cheaper than any pill that I could find on the street. I had been told over and over that I was wasting my money on pills, but I still had a little bit of sense to me, which lasted for about ten minutes this time, before I called my dealer back to accept his offer. "Okay, come pick me up. Make sure you take care of me, though." He said.

I did not have a choice. I could not find pills anywhere else, and I refused to go into withdrawal again. My back was against the wall. After we picked up the dope and got back to his house, he poured the pile of brown powder on his table. This was the first time that I had ever seen heroin with my own eyes. My heart was pounding. He proceeded to split the pile into two smaller lines. "You go first," I insisted.

"Bro, don't worry. It's just like a pill, but way stronger. It's gonna make you feel better."

He did not even hesitate to snort his pile of heroin. He assured me that it did not burn any more than snorting a pill, so I took the straw from him, leaned over the table and became a heroin addict. Just like that. What an $80 pill would do for me, $10 worth of heroin did the same. More even! I could not believe how long it took me to try this. How much money that I had wasted. To this very day, I still have not been able to come up with a proper way to describe the feeling. The pain, both physical and emotional, was gone. From that moment, I never did another pill again.

There was only one problem that I encountered. Everyone that I associated with did pills. I needed to find a new crowd. I needed other dope fiends. It did not take very long, however. Just like with pill heads, one connection led to another, and eventually, I would meet a man that would change my life. Let's call him Ron. Ron was older than me, probably in his middle to late forties, and he knew exactly what he was doing when it came to heroin. Once I found him, I knew that Ron was the only person that I needed in my life, so we formed a partnership. Ron had a consistent and reliable way to get money, all he needed was a ride. This was perfect because he had money, but no car. I had a car and no money. We had a perfect setup.

Every day for about a month, he would call me at around 7:30 a.m. so that we could start our day. The timing had something to do with the way that he was getting his money, which was normally about $70 a day. This was enough to get us a half gram of heroin that we would split. Every morning was the same, except for one. This one morning sticks out to me because, well, he did not call me. I needed him for his money so that I could get high. So, I called him at 7:30. No answer. I called again. Nothing. Frantically I tried to get ahold of him. 7:36, 7:41, 7:50, 7:54, 8:00, 8:02, 8:02, 8:02, 8:02, 8:03. Everyone told me that heroin was a lot more powerful and way cheaper than pills. They were right. The downside, however, is that the withdrawal from heroin is way worse. Unbearably worse.

I never once thought that something bad may have happened to him. I was just furious with him. Frantically, I rummaged through my parent's belongings, looking for something to take to the pawnshop. Nothing. Phone call after phone call I made, desperately trying to convince people to loan me some money. Nothing. I went an entire day with no drugs in my system, and it was the most miserable thing that I had ever experienced. I spent all day in the house, scheming about ways that I could somehow get money to get some dope. But I had no more resources. Even if I had found a way to get money, Ron was my only connection to get the drugs. I was screwed either way.

The day was horrible, but the night was worse. No sleep. Only sweating, aching bones, tight muscles, and non-stop moving around. It hurt to move, but I could not stop myself. After an entire 24 hours of torture, I was quickly motivated to get up and moving when I felt my phone vibrating. It was Ron. "Get up and come on," he said. Like nothing even happened. I wanted to cuss him out and really let him have it, but I got dressed and headed out to pick him up instead. Mentally, I felt better just knowing that I would feel better soon. Physically though, I threw up twice and could not stop shaking or moving around. I even had to have him drive because I was completely unable to.

After picking up the dope, we pulled into our usual parking spot where would get high before we would head back across the river to Kentucky. Ron split up what we had on a CD case. Normally, I would immediately lean over and snort mine so that I could feel better, but there was a battle going on in my head. Ron used needles to inject the heroin straight into his veins, and he had always told me just how much better it was. He told me that the high was more intense, and I would not have to do as much if I shot it. It would hit me faster and I would be able to save more for later. It had been tempting in the past, but I had never been this sick before. Ron finished his shot and looked over at me with a puzzled look on his face. "You okay, bud?" he asked. "You normally have half the pile up your nose by now."

I simply replied, "hit me."

I was desperate. I could not take the pain anymore. I could handle the withdrawal from pills, but this was too much.

"What? Are you sure?"

"Yes! Just hurry!" I demanded.

Until then, I had never really watched how he shot up. Even after a month or so of getting high with him, I had no idea how to do it. This time, I paid close attention. I watched as he put a small amount of heroin in his spoon. I studied as he drew up some water into the syringe and squirted it onto the dope. Then he flipped over the needle and used the plunger to mix the poison together. "Give me a cigarette," he said. I was annoyed that he chose that moment to smoke, but I did not argue. I handed him a cigarette. Instead of lighting it, he took the filter between his teeth and ripped off a piece of the cotton filter, balled it up, and stuck it on the end of the needle. Before I could even ask, he explained, "The cotton is so you do not suck up any chunks of heroin into the needle. You will either get a busted needle or it'll make you really sick."

With the heroin and the needle both prepped, he drew the mixture into the syringe and leveled it off. He really stressed to me the importance of making sure that all of the air was out of the syringe. "Too much air could blow your heart out. Now gimme your arm and make a fist."

I did as instructed. I watched as Ron carefully slid the needle through my skin and into my vein. He pulled back on the plunger just a little bit. "Always draw back on the plunger a little bit. You need to draw blood. That's how you know that you are in your vein."

Bullseye. He pushed down on the plunger, injecting the poison into me. The entire process took less than a minute, and within three seconds flat, I felt it. I felt a cool feeling in my throat, followed by a heavy, numb feeling that started in my legs and slowly making its way up through the rest of my body. My eyes got heavy and I smiled uncontrollably as I sank into my seat. I can still feel the feeling as I write this.

"A lot better than snorting it, huh?"

I do not even think that I said anything. The best way that I can explain it is, Heaven. This is what Heaven must feel like.

This is where the party really got crazy. One of Ron's neighbors was in a bad motorcycle accident, which was great news for Ron and me. He ended up getting a settlement for $50,000, which was split up over five weeks. Basically, we were getting $10,000 a week, and almost all of it was going to heroin. Ron and I both had leverage on this kid. Ron had some dirt on him, and I had my car. So, Ron got dope for keeping his mouth shut, and I got mine by being the taxi driver. It was a beautiful setup.

Let me put this into perspective a little bit for you. We had $10,000 a week. After we bought food, cigarettes, and gas, we had between $9,000 and $9,500 left over for heroin. The heroin that we were buying cost $120 per gram, which means that we were getting around 75 grams of heroin a week! Just between the three of us. Before this happened, Ron and I were getting between three and five grams a week, and that was plenty. Now, we were going through 75 grams between the three of us. Twenty-five grams a week per person. It is safe to say that none of us have any right still being alive. The fear of overdosing was enough to keep me from doing as much as them, though. Ron could handle it because he had been using heroin for a long time. The other kid was just a lucky idiot. He was out of control all of the time. Going out into public with him was embarrassing, to say the least. I, on the other hand, would sell some of mine. I just could not do as much as them, but I hung in there with them, that is for sure.

The thing about being a drug addict is that you do not plan too much for the future. We felt like kings during those few weeks, but none of us thought about how this kind of drug use was going to affect us once it was all over. We got spoiled. We lost a lot of the contacts that we had before the money came rolling in. We pushed our tolerance through the roof, and when the money finally ran dry, Ron and I had to start completely over. It was a very rough and dark time. Ron had lost his consistent source of $75 a day, so we started every day the same way that we went to bed... broke. Ron would kick off the day by panhandling and begging people for money. I would drop him off at the busiest street corner that we could find, then I would get to work. My job was to steal, pawn, and sell any and everything that I could. If it had any value at all, I was taking it. From different stores. From my parent's house. Maybe even from your house. If I could make a dollar, and it was not bolted to the ground, it was mine.

I started with what I had left, such as my Xbox, television, sports memorabilia, and coins. Everything that I had. Even my prized Pokémon cards. I had spent years searching and thousands of dollars collecting those cards. I ended up selling every single one of them for nine bucks. Then, after all of my things were gone, I moved on to my parent's belongings. They had all kinds of old stuff. Old stuff sometimes means valuable stuff. Then my dad's tools and DVDs. Then my mother's jewelry box. It was all mine. Actually, it was all the pawnshop's or the dope boy's stuff.

Then, I made the most amazing discovery. While I was partaking in my daily routine of scrummaging through my parent's belongings, I came across a blue, leather money bag. I did not have high hopes that there would be anything in it other than receipts, but

I opened it anyway. BOOM! The inside of the bag was glowing with green! Oh, the relief of hitting the jackpot was awesome. My first thought, my natural thought, was to take it all and split it between Ron and me. But then I thought, these were my parents. This is their money. Why should anyone other than me get any of this? So, I took $120 so that I could get a gram for myself, and I kept quiet. This way, I would have the rest of the money for myself in emergencies. What I did was use the money that Ron made from begging on the corner, and kept my money, well, my parents' money, to myself.

This brought up a new problem for me, though. I am now sitting on thousands of dollars, but I could not really spend any of it because then I would have to share it with my loyal partner, Ron. We had always used his connections, so I decided that I needed to find my own dope boy. "I am getting really tired of Ron using me for my car all of the time. He doesn't even like me," is what I told myself. Which was funny because I was using him just as much, if not more, than he was using me.

Although I did not know my own heroin dealer, I had been around long enough to know how to find one. All I had to do was sit at a gas station in Cincinnati long enough and one would eventually find me. So, that is what I did. Sure enough, I got a couple of phone numbers. I knew that I had to be careful, though. You always wanted to make sure that you found a guy that was willing to give

46

you a "tester" so that you knew what you were getting. Otherwise, you may end up getting drywall or even a rock from the parking lot. Unfortunately, none of them would let me try their stuff, and I was not desperate enough at that moment to cave in and risk it. New approach. I caught wind that a couple of people that I had used to use pills with were now doing heroin, too. I reached out to them in hopes that they would introduce me to their dealer. It took a while, but eventually, I was able to get the phone number. I now had my very own dope boy. That sounds pretty stupid, right? It was an exciting time for me, though.

With the knowledge that I had learned from Ron, access to a bag full of money, and my newly acquired heroin dealer, I began to drift away from Ron. I simply just did not need him anymore like I used to. But I had to take it easy. I could not take the money in mass amounts because I did not want my parents to notice that I was taking it. Also, I needed that money to last as long as possible. If I was going to cut Ron out of the trusted circle of friends, which now just included me, then I would be taking on all of the responsibility rather than only being in charge of driving. It was a chance that I was willing to take, so I limited myself to $120 a day, or about a gram.

My limit only lasted me three or four days, though. I am not exactly sure how much money I spent over those few days, but I do know that it was over $1,000. How do I know? My father told me. Just like any other day, I waited for my parents to leave for work.

47

Once they did, I walked upstairs to where the money was being kept. When I opened it this time, instead of finding my source of relief for the day, I found a note which read, "You better not be taking this money!" It was a shot straight to the heart. Not because I had been caught. Not because I had been stealing from my parents. Not because I knew that they could have definitely called the police on me for this. No. My only concern was, what am I going to do now?

    I did my best to avoid my parents after that, for I did not have the time nor energy to fight with them about the money missing. I held out as long as I could, but eventually, we had "the talk." There were a lot of tears and a lot of yelling. My father told me where the money came from. He was working as a hospice chaplain during this time. The company that he was working for gave him the money to spend on his patients for whatever they needed to make them comfortable such as food, a bed, television, or anything else that would make them smile. The money was for his dying patients, not his dying son. But no real heroin addict is going to care too much. My only thought was where my source of money was going to come from now. My parents just did not understand that I needed that money far worse than his terminal patients.

    I had reached a new point of desperation after this. I had sold a lot of my things before this and I was now running out of items to sell. All of the expensive things were already gone, such as my Xbox, games, and DVDs. The little things followed like the rest of my baseball cards. The only things that were left were the sentimental items that my family cherished the most. Things that could never be replaced again. My father's old wedding ring. My deceased grandfather's wedding ring. All of my mother's best jewelry. I took it all. Heroin called the shots. The well-raised son of a preacher had been completely taken over by the devil.

There was nothing left. I had taken everything of value in the house. Lies were the only thing that I could rely on how. Any excuse that I could think of in an attempt to get money from my parents. Oil change, doctor appointment, or gas and food money. When the lies did not work, I would find myself army crawling through the house while my parents were asleep to slip money out of my dad's wallet or my mom's purse, which they now kept next to them while they slept. If they slept at all, that is. This was short-lived, however. They no longer kept cash with them at all, and you cannot steal something that is not there. There was nothing left to steal. No more lies to tell. I was out of luck, and my parents were out of patience.

Intervention

I was unaware, but my parents had been doing some research during all of this and came across a law in the state of

49

Kentucky called Casey's Law. Casey's Law was created as a way to give loved ones of an addict the ability to have the addict court-ordered to go to rehab. Finally, once they got their resources together and had reached their end, they approached me about their intentions. All of a sudden, a strange and unfamiliar feeling came over me. A mix of fear and relief. There was probably about 30% of me that wanted to get help and move on with the rest of my life. The other 70% was scared to death of the withdrawal and would rather die than have to go through it. Also, if I did go through the withdrawal and got sober, I would then be forced to live with all of the terrible things that I had done to my family and friends for so many years. Unbearable withdrawal followed by a lifetime of guilt and shame... no, thanks. But what choice did I really have? This law was going to completely take my thoughts and arguments out of the equation.

  The first step to Casey's law was to see two different doctors. A primary care physician and a specialist of some sort. They would need to conclude that I did, in fact, need treatment for my addiction and sign the proper documentation for the judge. I lied to both doctors during their evaluation, but they both agreed that I did, in fact, need to go to rehab. The second step was the court date. After the proper documentation had been signed by the doctors, a date and time were set for my parents and me to appear in front of a judge. A few years of lying, stealing, and non-stop heroin use gave my parents a great case. The third step was a waiting game. The judge made the decision that I definitely needed to get into rehab and gave me a timeframe to get into detox to begin my treatment. The problem with this was that there was only one detox center in my area, which only had a total of 13 beds. Every single day I had to call this detox facility to see if there was a bed available. Side note, this is completely ridiculous for an active heroin addict to have to do this. I did not want to go to detox, but there was no way around it. The judge gave me clear direction to get into detox within two weeks or go to jail. Either way, I would be going through the torture of heroin withdrawal. On the bright side, though, I would at least be able to smoke cigarettes at the detox facility, so I kept calling. Every call was the same. I asked the same question and they gave me the same answer.

For weeks I called until I finally just gave up. I mean, I did not want to go anyway, so why was I trying to get in willingly? Little did I know, Alicia (my girlfriend at the time) was calling too, and one evening, their answer changed. I remember this night well. I was sitting in my parent's driveway, smoking a cigarette when my mother called me inside and told me to pack my things. Alicia had called the detox facility, then called my mom to inform her that my bed was available and that I had an hour to get there. My heart was pounding, but I had about $40 worth of heroin in my pocket. Now my mission was to somehow get away from my mom long enough to do it, but I worked my way to my bathroom to shoot up for seemingly, the final time. I was hoping that I would overdose from that shot, but instead, it seemed to have no effect on me at all. I slowly packed a few things, and we began our journey to detox.

That fifteen-minute drive went by quickly, and I felt like my life was over. My mind was racing, thinking about everything from beginning my new life to saying, "fuck this," and jumping out of the moving car. But, I did not run. I stayed in the car until we arrived and immediately got out to throw up. Every step toward the front door was harder to take than the last. My stomach got tighter with every inch. I was so scared, for I knew what tomorrow was going to feel like. I was feeling alright for the time being because of the shot that I took right before we left, but there would be no heroin in my diet tomorrow.

Throughout my intake process, I became calmer. I was looking at the handful of other patients who were already there and in withdrawal, and it was comforting to know that I was the only one there who was high. It was late in the evening when I finished the intake process, so we spent the next hour or so sitting and talking in the common room before we had to go to bed. I was able to find some motivation from my conversation with the other patients. I realized that if they could do it, then I could certainly do it as well. But then the next morning came and I had lost all motivation. I was in hell. From the second that I opened my eyes, reality hit me, and fear gripped me like it had never done before. There was absolutely no way that I was going to be able to do this, and I needed a way out.

Throughout all of the madness that was going on in my head, I was able to remember that one of the other patients mentioned that he had snuck a cell phone into the facility, which was definitely against the rules, but also definitely worth the risk. My mind was made up; I was leaving, so I asked the guy for his phone. "Man, yea. But make it quick," he said.

I agreed, although I knew that this was not going to be a quick or easy conversation. It was going to take some good lying and manipulating to get out of this one. I knew that my parents were completely out of the question, so I called Alicia. She answered the phone with a confused tone. She knew that I was not allowed to be using the phone. It was the policy that no detox patient was allowed to use the phone nor have any visitors.

"What do you want?" She asked.

"I'm ready to go," I replied. "After taking my vitals all night and observing me, they don't think that I need to be here. They need my bed to give to someone who actually needs it." This was the only lie that I could come up with that I thought would make any sense.

To my surprise, she actually agreed to come and get me. As I was packing my things into a trash bag, a couple of staff members came in to get me. They caught me packing and asked me for my phone. I told them that I did not have a phone. They responded with, "Then why did we just get a call from your girlfriend? She told us that she just got off the phone with you. Oh, and don't worry, you aren't going anywhere."

I could not believe that she would betray me like that. As I said, though, my mind was made up and nothing was going to keep me there.

"You guys can't keep me here," I responded.

"Matt, you are here under Casey's law. If you leave, there will be a warrant issued for your arrest. Think carefully about what you are doing. The police will eventually find you, and you will go to jail and end up right back here anyway. You might as well just stay."

I could hear what they were saying, and I knew that it was all true, but I did not listen one bit. I packed up my garbage bag and left. With no phone, no money, and nowhere to go, I headed my way down the main drag of Bellevue, Kentucky. Just thinking about what I was going to do. I needed a plan. Step one, get a ride. I decided to call my old friend Mike. The reason why I chose to call him was simple. His number was the only one that I had memorized. Step two, find a place to call him from. The main street in Bellevue was full of small businesses and family-owned shops, so I stepped into a small tanning salon and asked to use their phone.

"Mike, what's up?! You busy? Would you mind doing me a favor? I just graduated from rehab and need a ride home. Will you come scoop me up?"

After being betrayed by Alicia, rejected by my parents, having been informed that I now have an active warrant out for my arrest and having nowhere to go, finally some good news. "Yeah, man, I'll come get you," he replied.

Homeless, Hopeless & Suicidal

Now, step three. Find a way to get money. I waited for Mike to pick me up for over an hour. Realistically, it was about 12 minutes. But, when you are in withdrawal, everything is extreme. Even time. When he finally arrived, I had him drop me off at my parents' house. They were both at work, which was great for me because they would have definitely called the police on me. My only fear was that Alicia had called them to warn them that I was leaving detox. But still, no one was home, so I crawled into the house through the back window. In a hurry and in a panic, I grabbed my car keys (my parents' car keys, rather), and my parents' laptop, and left. I did not even say thank you to Mike for the ride or anything. I was dope sick and needed it to end as soon as possible. Throughout this entire process, my only focus was on getting some heroin so that

I could feel better. I was desperate. I did not realize the situation that I had just put myself into. But I continued on to the pawnshop to sell my parent's laptop and headed up to the dope boy.

Now that I was feeling better, where do I go? What am I going to do? As soon as I took the shot and was able to think clearly again, the realization of the situation that I just put myself in hit me hard. I am now homeless and officially on the run from the police. I have no friends. My family has disowned me. Literally, all that I had was three pairs of clothes, the car, and the hope that Alicia would not call the cops on me. The only thing that I could do was go to her workplace and find out. So that is what I did. When I arrived in the parking lot, there were some other employees outside smoking, so I asked one of them to ask Alicia to come outside when they went back in. I had never seen her so angry before. Of course, I got what I expected. A long lecture which I had prepared for by taking another shot of dope before she came outside. She broke it down for me by saying that I was now a fugitive, I was homeless, and that I was an idiot. Then I broke it down for her by saying I know, I do not care, and that I needed her paycheck. She gave me what she had. I somehow managed to always get her to do anything that I wanted. I feel bad about it now, for she just did not know what to do. It is difficult to find that line between loving and enabling an addict.

That evening, I took the money that I had left over from selling the laptop and combined it with the money that Alicia gave me so that I could get as much dope as I could. I knew it was going to be a long night. It was the fall and it was starting to get cold. The only place that I had to sleep was my car, which was risky since I was hiding from the police. There was no doubt that my parents had reported the car stolen. All it would take for me to get caught would be for someone to walk by and see me sleeping in my car then report me. I had to find somewhere safe, so I decided to park in the emergency room parking lot at one of the hospitals in the area. Out of all of the places that I could have gone, I figured that the hospital would be the safest. If someone walked by the car and saw me sleeping in the back seat, I could always just lie to them and say that I have a loved one in the hospital and that I just needed to get away from the stress for a while. I backed the car into a spot with a tree behind it. That way, my license plate was not showing.

I slept in the back seat of that car for a couple of weeks. Every once in a while, I would use some of Alicia's paycheck to get a hotel room so that I could sleep comfortably, get a shower, and eat something. Other than that, all of the money went to cigarettes, gas, and heroin. A two-week paycheck lasted me two days. After that, I was on my own again, to steal and sell.

Those two weeks were just a blur of constant fear. I wanted to die, and each day that went by, I wanted to die even more. I knew that the cops would find me. It was only a matter of time. My car would be reported, or I would get caught stealing. Either way, I was in no way willing to go through the withdrawal. Nor was I willing to be sober because then I would have to live with the shame and guilt of doing what I have been doing for so long. There was only one other way out of this, so I made the decision that when the police finally did find me, that would be the time that I would kill myself. My best idea of accomplishing this was to take a bunch of sleeping pills. I have wanted to fall asleep and never wake up for quite a while now. Maybe I could finally make it happen. So, one night I went to the store to steal once again, but this time it was not for something to sell. It was for the pills that would put me to sleep for good.

From that night on, I kept a cigarette pack full of different types of sleeping pills in my pocket at all times. When the police found me, I would take every single one of them. I was serious about it too. I even wrote my parents an apology/goodbye letter and left it in the car. The end was drawing closer.

As if things could not get any worse, the car that I had been living in died, and it was getting to be very cold out at nighttime. To make matters even worse, my windows were down in the back seat when the car crapped out. I had nothing left to do other than to rely on Alicia to bail me out again. I begged her to allow me to live in her car, but the sad part of this was that I was actually happy about it. Her car was an upgrade compared to mine. It was bigger, and the police were not looking for her car. There was one problem, though. Her grandmother. Alicia had been living in a hotel with her grandmother to keep her company due to some family issues that they were going through at the time. Normally, I would not have cared, but her grandmother knew about me and the entire story. She promised to have me arrested if she was ever given the chance, so I had to be careful.

I was only in my new home for about a month when "it" happened. The police finally showed up. I had the car for the day while Alicia was at work. After her shift, I went and picked her up just as I always would. When we arrived back at the hotel, we sat in the car and chatted for a little bit. She then went inside, and a few moments later, I look up and see two Florence police cruisers pull into the parking lot and park directly behind me. My heart drops. The police officers approach the car and begin to ask me some questions while I was still sitting in the back seat. Then Alicia comes back out of the hotel to ask the officers what is going on. The time had come. While both of the officers were distracted by Alicia, I reached into my pocket, dumped the entire cigarette pack of sleeping pills into my hand, and threw them into my mouth. I had about 80 pills and I managed to get most of them in. Then I washed them all down with one big gulp of an old pop that was in the cupholder. Suddenly, the fear of the police, jail, and the withdrawal was all gone, for I knew that in just a few hours, I would be dead. I calmly stepped out of the car, placed my hands behind my back, got into the back of one of the police cars, and we headed to the Boone County Jail. I remember pulling up to the jail and walking into one of the holding cells, but after that, nothing.

It was a Sunday night when I was arrested and sent to the Boone County Jail. Three days would go by before I was woken up by a *Kenton County* corrections officer. I was transferred to Kenton County because that was the county that my warrant was issued from. I have no recollection of the move. When the corrections officer woke me up, he asked, "Do you know where you are?"

"Yeah. I'm at the hospital," I replied.

I had no idea what was going on, where I was, or what had happened, but surely if I was still alive, I must be at the hospital, right? Then the officer held up the pink uniform, which read "Kenton County Detention Center" on the back of it. It was a very strange feeling. I was mad that I was alive. But, I was also mad that I was in jail and not in the hospital. Nobody did a thing to try to save my life. I was clearly overdosing on something, but for some reason, the officers thought that just throwing me in a cell and checking in on me once every other hour would be sufficient.

For the next eight days, I spent my time in "the hole" on suicide watch. My cell consisted of a tiny concrete room, a bed also made of concrete raised about three inches off of the ground (it basically was the ground), and a special edition toilet/sink/water fountain combo. I was completely stripped of my clothes and was given a small tear-resistant blanket. The cell was freezing cold, and the blanket they provided me with was only around four feet in length. To keep my feet warm, I wrapped toilet paper around them to make socks. Embarrassing, I know, but I cannot stress how cold it was in there. I was allowed no eating utensils. My food was served to me in a Styrofoam box, so I had to improvise and tear a piece of the box off and use it as a spoon. The only other thing that I had was time, uncertainty, and my thoughts. Oh, and lots of sleep, which was constantly being disrupted by the guards opening and shutting my window, or the other inmates who felt determined to be as loud and obnoxious as they could.

 My first experience with pepper spray also took place in the hole, and I will never forget it. The inmate in the cell next to me was having an extra emotional evening... or morning. We never knew what time it was, for there were no windows to see if it was light or dark outside. For quite some time, the inmate would kick the door to his cell and yell profanity at the guards and whoever else would listen. Finally, after failing to accomplish whatever it was that he was trying to accomplish, he made one last attempt by throwing feces all over his cell. This got the guards' attention. It was like something from television. Four or five guards stacked up in front of his cell. The lead guard opened the inmate's window and filled the cell with pepper spray. Wow, pepper spray sucks! It quickly made its way into my cell. It took my breath away. The feeling of it in my throat was like I just swallowed a box of thumbtacks. That was definitely the highlight of my stay in the hole. The upside was, however, that it was good entertainment and passed the time.

Finally, after eight of the longest days of my life, freezing to death in the concrete cell, using toilet paper for socks, the social worker that was assigned to me determined that I was no longer a threat to myself. At last, I was moved to a dorm and given back my clothes. The dorm that I was moved to held 72 inmates. It was just one big open room. There were nine cubicles on either side of the dorm, each holding four "racks" (jail slang for beds). There was a big television in the center of the room which stayed on almost all day depending on the mood of the corrections officer. In the very front of the dorm were two smaller rooms. One room held sinks and toilets. The other was the shower room, which was literally just four showerheads hanging off of the walls. Zero privacy in either room. In the back of the dorm room was a small, fenced-in basketball court. This would have been great if it was not November. It was freezing outside. I adapted to the change of environment fairly well. There were plenty of times that I would have rather been back in the hole, though. At least it was quiet in there. But it was nice having some human contact. I had not had any real contact with another person in months other than Alicia.

During my time in the dorm, I began to feel a little bit better physically. I was also able to find out what happened during those three missing days after my attempted suicide, and apparently, I was not just sleeping as I had thought. A couple of guys that were in my dorm were in charge of cleaning the hallways of the jail. One of them told me that I was constantly shouting all sorts of gibberish along with trying to convince him to let me out of my holding cell so that I could escape. One of the corrections officers who was in charge of watching me during my intake process said that I was having conversations with an imaginary fly. He also informed me that I was hitting on the lady who was doing my intake paperwork, asking her out on dates, and trying to talk her into letting me go so that I could take her out on a date. Another officer, who I used to go to high school with, told me that he witnessed me reaching my hand into my toilet. When he asked me what I was doing, I replied with "my needles are in here. I need my needles."

So, from what I gathered, my missing three days were filled with hallucinations. I have been able to remember some of it as time has passed.

Although I was adapting well to the situation, I was still carrying all of the weight from what I had put my family through. I will never forget this. It was visitation day and my name was called, but I was not expecting anyone to be visiting me. I continued to walk up to the television screen and picked up the phone, which turned the monitor on. My parents were at the other end. I tried my very best to keep the tears from falling from my eyes. I could not believe that they still loved me. The visit was a short ten minutes, but during the allotted time, they brought me up to speed on what was going on with my case. They told me that they were still going to move forward with Casey's law, and I cheerfully agreed. I mean, the withdrawals were over. I tried to kill myself, but that obviously did not work. So, since I was still alive, I might as well go to treatment and try to learn how to live. They also told me that they found the car that I had stolen from them and the goodbye/suicide letter that I left them. I could not believe it, but they told me that they were preparing for the worst and had already picked out the clothes that they were going to have me buried in. No parent should ever have to make those kinds of preparations for their child.

 I spent a total of three weeks in Kenton County Detention Center before I was shipped back to Boone County Jail. I was transferred to Boone County on a Monday morning, where I waited to go to court. Since I was on the run for a couple of months, the judge had to order me back to rehab for a second time. Fortunately, he did, but this time he made me wait in jail for a bed to open up at the treatment center that I was being sent to. I did not blame him for keeping me in jail this time, for I had not given him any reason at all to believe that I would go willingly since I ran the last time. The only downside was that I did not know how long it would be before my bed would be ready. I was told that it could be anywhere from one day to up to three months, but, I knew that I was fortunate to not only have a second chance to go to rehab, but a second chance at life. At that moment, I was willing to sit in jail as long as I had to.

To my surprise, when I called my parents from jail the next day, they told me that my bed would be ready that following Monday. Only six more days to go! It was a long, yet easy six days. I was excited to finally get out of jail and begin to rebuild my life. The excitement made time go slow, but Boone County Jail was set up differently than Kenton County. Instead of being in one massive dorm with 70 other inmates, I was in a ten-man cell. The inmates that I shared a cell with were actually a great group of guys. They were all Spanish and shared everything with each other, including me. They shared coffee with me, food, they gave me socks and a t-shirt. They even taught me how to play Chinchon, which is a card game much like Rummy. Their generosity had a great impact on my remaining time in jail.

A Second Chance

Finally, Monday. I woke up for breakfast, but instead of going back to sleep like I usually did, I stayed awake and anxiously waited for the officer to come and get me from my cell. After an eternity of waiting (about two hours), the officer finally arrived and called my name. I quickly gathered my things, said my goodbyes to the other inmates, and thanked them for making my time easier, and then I left. I cannot describe the feeling that I had when I was released from jail into the arms of my parents. I had not seen them face to face in months. I had not hugged them even longer than that, so for those few seconds, the world stood still. I only had two hours to get to the treatment center, though, so we had to get moving. I had a lot to do before I went. First thing was first. I was in desperate need of a haircut. My hair looked similar to Johnny Depp's in the movie Sweeney Todd. Next, some real food. Regardless of what you may have heard, the food that they serve you in jail really is not that great. Actually, to be completely honest, dog treats would have been just fine with me. After I had my fill, we rushed home so that I could pack up a few things to take with me to rehab. It was a really fast two hours.

I was excited, ready, and willing until we pulled into the parking lot, that is. Once we parked, fear was all that I felt. The familiar thought of running away crossed my mind. Or, maybe I could convince my parents to change their minds. I mean, I did just spend the last month in jail, so was spending the next nine to twelve months in a long-term treatment facility really necessary? I continued to try and think of a good argument or some sort of plan all the way to the front door, but I could not. I did not say a word. God was clearly doing for me what I could not do for myself at that moment. Then, God took it one step further (He likes to show off from time to time). As I sat on the couch, going through the intake process and filling out paperwork, I recognized a voice. It was a very familiar voice. I stopped filling out the paperwork and looked up. There stood my best friend, Kyle, staring at me.

Kyle and I went back to when I was thirteen years old. When we first met, he was the "cool guy." He was a skater with tattoos and gauges in his ears. Kyle was in a couple of bands, listened to loud music, and skipped school regularly. He was pretty much the type of kid that I tried to avoid as much as possible. But, drugs will take you to some funny places because he eventually became my best friend. We used to hang out in the woods with a group of other kids from our neighborhood. Our gang would hide out in the woods and drink stolen beer and smoke pot, but Kyle and I eventually branched off from the rest of the group because we enjoyed getting high more than the others. Our drug use progressed at about the same rate, so we began to seek out cocaine, Percocet, Vicodin, and Oxycontin. At one point, we began to separate from each other because our drug use was tearing us apart. But, after we had both turned to heroin, we found our way back to each other from time to time. We would become "partners in crime" in order to get what we needed, but our friendship was nearly non-existent. He had his own ways to get heroin, and I was hanging around Ron most of the time to get my own. Regardless of the way our relationship ended, it was a huge relief to hear his voice and see his face in the lobby of the treatment center. Honestly, I do not know if I was more relieved for his sake or my own, but either way, we were together again, except this time, we were sober.

The rehab that I was sent to was a long-term inpatient program, and I needed every bit of it. The program was split up into five parts: S.O.S (Safe Off the Streets), Motivational Track 1, Motivational Track 2, Phase 1, and Phase 2.

S.O.S was the first part of the program and lasted for about the first three weeks. During that time, I was required to wear blue scrubs, I was not allowed to leave the facility for any reason, use the phone, or have any visitors. The point of all of that was to give me time to settle in and get me grounded in the program. It was important for me to use that time to focus on myself only. The days consisted of waking up at 5:45 a.m. to eat breakfast. After breakfast, we were given some simple chores to do, such as cleaning our bathrooms, sweeping the floor, and taking out the trash. The rest of the day was crammed full of classes and Alcoholics Anonymous meetings. The classes were normally open discussions about our experience in treatment so far, stories about our drug use and sobriety, and education about treatment. S.O.S was exhausting but full of information. It was also a great time to build new friendships with the twelve to fifteen other guys that were in S.O.S with me.

Motivational Track 1 and 2 were pretty much exactly the same. Like S.O.S, the days were filled with classes and meetings. The major difference was that I was now allowed to use the phone and go home on weekends from 8:00 to 4:00. This was a great, yet stressful, time. My family were not addicts. I was excited to be sober, but I found it to be extremely difficult to talk to my parents. For most of my life, I spent my time hiding from my parents and lying to them about who I was with, where I was, or what I was doing. Now that I was no longer doing those things, I realized that I had no idea how to act like a son. I just could not relate to them. Before I had gotten sober, I had spent all of my time with other people who used drugs. Then, I was sent to jail to hang out with other drug addicts and criminals twenty-four hours a day, seven days a week. After jail, I was sent to rehab with 118 other addicts. My experience with "normal people" was extremely limited. Luckily for me, and for my family, this is exactly what Phase 1 was for.

Phase 1 of the program ranged anywhere from three to six months long and was the bread and butter of the entire program. Phase 1 dealt primarily with the twelve steps of Alcoholics

Anonymous. They broke down the steps and made each one into a worksheet in order to simplify them. This is where I really got to take a look at myself. Not only that, but it also showed me just how much my actions affected other people. I carried around the guilt for hurting my parents, but I also felt like the victim for my circumstance. It was the van driver's fault. It was the doctor's fault. My family just did not understand me. My friends turned their backs on me. It was always someone else's fault other than my own. But Phase 1 showed me that this was not the case at all. It was all me. I caused all of my own stress. I put myself into all of the dangerous situations that I had been in. I was the one who pushed everyone else out of my life, not the other way around. My actions caused me to live in the back seat of a car. I was the one who lost everything, and absolutely nothing was taken from me. What an eye-opener to find out that I, the infamous Matt Peterson, was the one at fault.

My friendships with a lot of the other clients strengthened while I was in Phase 1. Kyle was always my "go-to guy" whenever I needed someone to talk to, but I was lucky enough to meet and create friendships with a lot of other guys. Perhaps the most influential friendships that I made came from an Alcoholics Anonymous meeting. Since the entire program that I was in was based around Alcoholics Anonymous, we were required to go to at least five meetings outside of the treatment facility every week. I would go to different meetings, but one, I made a point to go to. It was my home group. The meeting that I committed to attend on a regular basis. The meeting was called The Big A, and it met once a week on Wednesday evenings. This particular meeting is where my sponsor and my grand sponsor attended regularly and were a huge part of my journey in recovery. After the meeting was over, a group of guys from the treatment center and I would swing by Northern Kentucky University to play volleyball for an hour or two before we had to be back to the facility. That was the tradition, and we had a ton of fun. I had found that being sober was great. Learning about myself and figuring out who I was, was great. But, it all meant nothing if I was not able to have a little fun while I was doing it. I mean, what would be the point of learning to live life if I was not able to enjoy it?

    Phase 1 was not always a good time, though. Throughout the program, I got attached to a lot of the guys that I went through it with. But, not all of us made it. Some of them would decide that they no longer needed treatment anymore, so they would make the decision to leave without completing the program. Others would be arrested because they would break a major rule of the treatment center or have an outstanding warrant. Over half of the clients were sent to the treatment center by the department of corrections. Therefore, if they were kicked out of the program from breaking the rules, the staff would call the police to come and take them back to jail. Others relapsed. Regardless of the reason, it was never easy to see a friend leave. Of course, I missed them after they would leave, but I feared for their safety even more. I will never forget my first experience with the death of a fellow client. His name was Jacob Fox. Jake was the peer mentor who was in charge of going through the intake process with me when I first arrived. He was finished with the program but had decided to volunteer as a peer mentor to help other clients make their way through the program. He was a great person to talk to, and he had helped me out a lot at the beginning of my treatment. But, one day, Jake decided to steal a box of latex gloves out of the kitchen so that he could do tattoos on the weekends to make himself some money. Well, this was one of those major rules that the facility had. No stealing. But, he did, and he was caught. Normally, this would result in the client being kicked out to the treatment center and arrested. His punishment, however, was far worse than that. Instead of kicking him out, the staff decided to completely restart him in the program, which meant that he would go back to S.O.S and have to spend nearly another year in the program. He agreed at first, but after just a couple of days, he left. Exactly three days after he left, he was dead. Almost all of his support group was in the treatment center. Now that he was on his own, he relapsed, overdosed, and passed away. It is amazing how such a small slip, like latex gloves, can lead an addict straight to the grave.

Finally, after about nine months, it was my time to transition into Phase 2. This was the end of the program. During Phase 2, I was required to get a job, and that was basically all there was to do. I still had to make sure that I attended my five Alcoholics Anonymous meetings a week, but other than that, my only concern was to work and start planning to move out. Finding a job was actually very easy for me. While I was still in Phase 1, I took a trip to my old job, a Tex Mex restaurant. While I was eating, my old boss approached me at my table. I had done a lot of pretty bad things during my employment there in the past, so I was nervous to see him. What was I going to say? What was he going to say? The only rational thing that he could say to me was to remind me about all of the bad decisions that I had made while I worked there and then tell me that I am no longer welcome to eat there. In fact, he actually called the police on me once and had me arrested for selling pills to one of the other employees. So, when he reached my table, I stood up, shook his hand, and had every intention of leaving. I let him take the lead in the conversation. To my surprise, he never asked me to leave. Actually, quite the opposite. Instead of banishing me from the property, he offered me my old job back. He stated that the kitchen had been struggling lately and that he really needs the extra help. He even commended me for my honesty about everything that had happened and for doing what I needed to do in order to get my life back on track. This, my friends, is an example of how God was working in my life.

I started working at the restaurant the same day that I transitioned into Phase 2. I worked as much as I could. It felt really good to be doing something productive again. But if I was not working, I was hanging out with my friends at the center, going to meetings, or hanging out with my son. My son, Christian Green Peterson, was born while I was in rehab, and what a huge blessing he is! Alicia was pregnant before I went into treatment, but at the time, I had no plans at all for being alive to be a father to him. I surely was going to be dead before then. So, Christian holds a very special place in my heart because of that.

My original plan was to stay in the center until I had reached one full year of sobriety. That would have been November 12, 2012. The temptation to leave simply became too great. I had no other obligation at the center, and I felt like I needed to be at home to help take care of my five-month-old son. Sometime in August, I began the exiting process to move out. The process was two weeks from start to finish and involved filling out a "plan of action" packet and explaining it to the rest of the Phase 2 clients in a group setting. If they all approved, then they would vote, and I would be allowed to move back home. As I explained my plan of action, which included the address of where I would be moving to, where I would be working, and what I was going to be doing in order to ensure my sobriety, I was given a lot of positive and motivating feedback from the other clients. I was told that during my time in treatment I had been a "model client" and that if any one of us would be able to remain sober that it would be me.

Back To The Real World

The night that I moved out was an emotional one for sure. I had spent so much time away from home that I thought that I would be more excited to finally go back. But to be honest, I was really going to miss rehab. That may sound weird, but I had not had any sober friends before, and nearly all of them lived there. It was hard to leave my friends, but what made things even harder was the phone call that I had received as I was packing up my belongings. My grandfather had not been doing very well over the past few years, but he had gotten a lot worse recently. The phone call was from my mother, telling me that my grandfather had passed away. She explained to me that they were eating at the dining room table. After he had finished eating his meal, he stood up, walked to the living room, and collapsed face down into his favorite chair. I was heartbroken, for I had not spent very much time with him over the years because of my drug use and did not really have the time to see him much since I had gotten sober because of the busy schedule of rehab. The treatment center taught me a lot of things, but one thing they did not touch on was how to deal with the death of a family member. As I look back on it all, I should have taken his passing as a sign. As I said, I was originally planning to move out on my one-year anniversary. I find it very ironic that he passed away on the day that I decided to move out. But, I was committed to move out, so I did.

My first week living back at home with my family was very difficult. Not only did I have to deal with the passing of my grandfather, but for nearly the entire past year, I had been living on someone else's schedule. Between jail and rehab, I had been told when to wake up, when to go to sleep, when to eat, what to eat, when I could watch television, what I was allowed to watch on television and when I was allowed to have free time. Being told what to do and when to do it for so long was definitely frustrating, so being set free from all of it sounded great to me at the time, but once I was able to think for myself and come up with my own schedule, I realized that I had no idea what to do with my time. I was working full time, but I did not do much else of anything. Not knowing what to do with my free time, I just sat around and did my best to relax. The time was very stressful, however. Once I left rehab and moved back home, I was immediately forced to become the son that I had never been. But, I did not know how to do that. Also, I was forced to be a father to my six-month-old son. I did not know how to do that, either.

The following weeks did not get any easier for me. My son, Christian, was only six months old and had already been hospitalized for pneumonia three times. On the third time that we took him to Children's Hospital, the nurse was doing her normal checks on him when she recommended that we get an x-ray of his chest to confirm the pneumonia once again. We went through the motions of having the x-ray done and returned back to our room. One more time, the nurse listened to his heart and his lungs, but this time, she heard something that none of the other nurses or doctors heard. Something was wrong with his heart. It was unclear what the problem was, but we had plenty of time to find out. We ended up staying in the hospital for two weeks. His pneumonia was pretty bad, so they wanted to keep him hooked up to the I.V. and run tests on his heart, so they could figure out what was wrong. After blood work, EKGs, x-rays, and an MRI, we finally found out what was wrong with my sweet boy. He was born with two holes in his heart, a ventricular septal defect, and an atrial septal defect. The heart is divided up into four chambers with walls separating them. The holes in his heart were in the walls which divided his heart. These holes caused blood to flow between the chambers and also allowed oxygen-rich blood to mix with oxygen-poor blood. This was also the reason why he was getting pneumonia. The doctor explained to us just how lucky that he was that they were able to identify the problem. He said that Christian would not have lived to two years old if they had not found the holes. This news was devastating. He was only six months old! He was innocent and did not deserve this.

  I grew angry with God when we found out the news. I was newly sober, fresh out of rehab, my grandfather just passed away, and then I find out that my son was born with two holes in his heart and was going to have open-heart surgery in an attempt to repair his heart. But wait, it gets better. Children's Hospital is a great hospital, but it is located just two streets away from my primary dope dealer, and dead smack in the middle of the rest of the dealers that I would go to in a pinch. I was under a lot of stress during this time, and I was not doing any recovery-related activities. My son needed me more than ever, and now was my time to be there. So, I stopped going to meetings. I stopped hanging out with my friends. I stopped playing volleyball at the university. And, I slowly stopped calling my sponsor. I was putting myself into a really bad place, I knew that I needed to continue to at least go to meetings; I needed support more than ever. But, I could not seem to justify leaving my son's side.

The rest of the time that we were in the hospital was full of more tests, planning, and scheduling. The priority during this time was to get Christian healthy enough so that he could have the surgery. But after two long weeks, we were finally able to go home to relax a bit before we would have to go back for the surgery. I did my best to pick back up where I left off, but it was hard. My friends in recovery began to talk to me differently and expressed that they were afraid that I was going to relapse. I was honest with them about not going to meetings or anything over the last two weeks, and this worried them. I could not seem to have a normal conversation with anybody. They just kept telling me what I was doing wrong, what I should be doing instead, and asking me if I was alright. Of course, I thought that I was. I was just being a good father. It was clear that they just did not understand that my son needed me. He was literally dying. What kind of father would I be if I left him to go to a meeting or to hang out with my friends? To me, that would make me a bad father. To everyone else who cared about me, I would have been doing what I needed to do in order to remain sober. Unfortunately, that was their concern, not mine.

Over the next couple of weeks before returning to the hospital, I returned to my meetings and attended my aftercare classes. They felt different now. I felt like everyone looked at me differently since I had not been to a meeting in two weeks. I felt like a suspect. Before my absence, I wanted to go to meetings. I wanted to continue learning and growing. I wanted to be sober. Now, the meetings felt more like a responsibility and an inconvenience. But, I still went back because I knew that it was what I was supposed to do. I went to at least one meeting every day until the day we had to go back to the hospital for another extended stay. On the day that we went back to the hospital, everything stopped once again. It was a very stressful and emotional day. I think the worst part of it all was the fact that my baby boy had no idea what was about to happen to him. He was a happy kid, and he had no clue at all that, in just a couple of hours, he was going to have his chest ripped open. I felt so bad for him. Man, I will never forget that day. I remember carrying him back to the operating room for anesthesia. When we arrived in the room, a nurse explained the process of how they were going to get him to sleep. I do not think that I listened to a single word that that nurse said. I kept my focus on Christian and fighting to keep the tears from falling. After the nurse was done with his explanation, he put the mask on Christian's face, and while I was holding him, he fell asleep. As soon as he was asleep, I began to cry, for I did not know if I was ever going to be able to see or hold him again.

For the next four hours, all I did was think about the worst possible outcome. I did whatever I could to stay busy. I took a walk around the hospital, played games on my phone, I even read some of the magazines that they had in the lobby. Anything that I could do in order to keep a hold on my sanity. Finally, Christian's name was called over the speaker. Weaving through the waiting area, I reached the front desk where the surgeon was waiting. Christian made it through the surgery just fine and was being moved to recovery where we could see him. My family and I quickly rushed to the recovery floor and walked into his room. I was extremely relieved that he made it through the surgery okay, but I was not at all prepared for the sight that awaited me inside of the recovery room.

I remember walking into his room and almost immediately walking back out. I tried my best to hold back the tears. He was completely lifeless. There were so many tubes, wires and machines hooked up to him that I could hardly see any of his body. I could not think of one good reason why he had to go through this.

We were in the hospital for another two weeks while he was recovering from his surgery, and just like the last time, I did not go to any meetings or anything else that had to do with my sobriety. I did call my sponsor a couple of times, but I stopped doing that, too, because he kept preaching at me to get to a meeting or do this or do that. My only focus was on my son. I had not experienced relapse before. Since this was my first time ever being sober, I did not know how to handle situations such as this one without using some sort of chemical. In the past, I would use events like this one as an excuse to get high, but now that I was not getting high anymore, what was I supposed to do? The natural thing for me to do was to be a father to Christian. You know, like any normal person would do. The thing is, though, is that I am not a normal person. I am an addict, and I was putting myself into a very dangerous situation. I did not see it, but my sponsor did. He warned me of what could potentially happen if I did not take care of myself, but I felt confident in myself. I felt like I was doing the right thing.

Relapse

Two days before Christian was due to be discharged from the hospital, I left to go to get us some ice cream from a shop that was just a couple of blocks away from the hospital. I pulled into the parking space and proceeded to the door. Before I could get inside, I heard a term yelled in my direction that I had not heard in eleven months. "Boy!" But he was not calling me "boy." He was referring to heroin. Instead of ignoring him and continuing on with my ice cream mission, I turned around and acknowledged the guy who was trying to get my attention.

"Hop in, man. I got something for ya."

"I'm good, man," I replied

"Come on. I got a tester for you right here."

"I've been off the stuff for almost a year. I'm good. Thanks, though."

"Aight, keep it up, then."

I was so proud of myself. For the first time ever, I was able to turn down heroin. And free heroin at that! I just proved to myself that I was over it. I was fine, just like I thought. And the best part, I was able to call my sponsor and say, "I told ya so!" I encountered an unexpected problem, though. After my run-in with the dope boy and being that close to my long-lost love, heroin, I could not seem to get it out of my mind. Yes, I turned it down and I was proud of myself that I was able to do that, but I began to obsess over it. For the next 24 hours, I could not stop myself from thinking about getting high. I had not contacted my dope boy for nearly a year, but it was clear to me that all I had to do was be a young white guy in Cincinnati and I would be able to get it. The next night, that is exactly what I did. I told my family that I was going to a meeting, but instead, I went out hunting for some heroin.

It only took me about an hour to find. I was amazed at how easy it was to get. Even after being out of the game for the last year and not having any contacts. I was excited and scared at the same time. Briefly, I tried to talk myself out of it, but not too hard. My house was empty, so I decided to go there. I drove fast, and when I finally arrived, I rushed downstairs to my bathroom where I used to get high. Just like clockwork, I did what I had been doing for years. I grabbed a spoon, dumped just a little bit of powder into the spoon, and filled up the needle with water. I shot the water into the spoon and stirred up the mixture. The whole time, my heart was racing, and I began to sweat. I continued to ask myself if this was a good idea, but I could not talk myself out of it. The urge was too strong. So, I drew the poison up into the syringe, stuck the needle into my vein, and pressed down slowly onto the plunger. Even now as I write this, I can feel it. The familiar sting in my arm. The warm, heavy feeling in my legs. My chest and arms becoming numb. Oh, how I missed it.

Physically, I felt incredible. Mentally, however, I was torn between "What the hell did I just do" and "Holy shit this was a great idea." I felt great, but I was also terrified because I remembered how bad I used to be. I remembered living in the back of a car and I remembered being beat down to the point of suicide. There was no way that I was going to get back to that point again. Just like many other heroin addicts that I knew, I had full intentions of controlling it. This time, I was starting from the beginning, so I convinced myself that I would be able to use heroin successfully... whatever that means.

I gave it one hell of a try, but my use progressed at a rapid pace, and within just a couple of weeks, I found myself slipping money out of Alicia's purse again. I began to lie again in order to get money from my parents. Alcoholics Anonymous was by far my best lie. It was the most positive thing that I had in my life, and my parents knew that a group of us would go out for dinner before or after the meeting. Sometimes we would go bowling or out to play putt-putt. Anytime that I would ask for money to do these things, the answer was always yes. Of course, I never did any of these things. I stopped going to meetings and I stopped talking to my friends who were still sober. I used every penny on cigarettes and heroin. It was ironic, really. The group of people that I used to help keep me sober were now the same group of people that I was using to get me high. It did not take long before I ended up right back where I left off. My circumstances weren't as bad this time around, but I stole everything from my family once again, split my family in two and became physically addicted, mentally bankrupt, and spiritually fucked. Luckily for me, although I did not see this as a blessing at the time, my parents were smarter now. They had been going to Al-Anon meetings over the past year in an attempt to learn how to deal with me as a heroin addict and how to cope for their own sake. They were able to meet some great people who were going through the same thing as they were. They were able to find the difference between loving and enabling me. They did research on different ways that I could get help. Honestly, I fully expected them to file Casey's Law on me again, but they never did. Instead of sending me back to rehab, like they probably should have done, they talked me into going to see a doctor in Ohio who could prescribe me Suboxone. At the time, Suboxone was still fairly new in the battle against addiction. Basically, it was a medication that helps opiate addicts with the withdrawal symptoms and also blocks the effects of opiates while the medicine is in your system. If an addict was actively taking Suboxone and attempted to get high on opiates, instead of getting the euphoric high, they would immediately go into precipitative withdrawal. I was on the fence about how I felt about taking Suboxone. To me, I would just be trading one drug for another. Instead of buying the drug I wanted illegally, I would now be buying a drug that I did not want, legally. It was a conspiracy. But, regardless of how I felt about it, I decided to give it a try anyway. My addiction was taking everything from me, and I did not want to die. There was a catch, though. In order for the Suboxone to work, I had to be in withdrawal at the time that I went to see the doctor. He told me over the phone how important it was for me to have all opiates out of my system. If not, I would go straight into withdrawal and possibly need to be hospitalized. A full day with no heroin? No way! I could not even go for four hours without using. Like I said, it was a conspiracy, so I took my last shot of heroin at around 2:00 in the morning, just six hours before my doctor's appointment.

That morning I woke up to no heroin, and I was completely miserable. Any confidence that I had that the Suboxone would work was gone. All willingness that I had to give the doctor a chance disappeared. I felt hopeless, but it seemed as if the doctor was my only shot at feeling better, so I went. The entire drive there I spent trying to fight and argue my way out of it, but my words fell on deaf ears. It was really frustrating, actually. For years, I had been able to talk my way out of nearly anything, but now, I could not even get them to acknowledge me. My parents did their homework, and now they knew exactly what to do in these types of situations, which was **DO NOT LISTEN TO ME.**

It was clear that I was not going to be able to talk my way out of this one, but I had one more trick up my sleeve. When we arrived at the doctor's office, I ran inside and locked myself in the bathroom. This was my last defense. My only plan now was to stay in that bathroom and throw a fit until they were too embarrassed to stay any longer. Forty minutes go by when I realize that was not going to work either. With no more ideas left, I had no choice but to emerge from the bathroom and see the doctor. I do not remember the conversation that the doctor and I had. I was so closed off that I did not hear a thing that he said to me. Through the entire process, I just kept thinking to myself that the Suboxone better work! That medication was my only chance to get the withdrawal over with. My focus was to get in and get out as quickly as possible so that I could get to the pharmacy to fill my prescription.

Once we reached the pharmacy, a new problem unfolded. My insurance did not cover the cost of the Suboxone and it was pretty expensive. The funny part was that, for some reason, my parents thought that I was going to be paying for the prescription. Yeah, right! Show me a heroin addict that has an extra $500 just laying around and I will show you a heroin addict who is the exception to the rules of addiction! Of course, my parents came up with the money so that I could fill the prescription.

I had now been in withdrawal all morning and was feeling a little bit more optimistic about the medication working for me. It had to work. I remembered the doctor's warning about waiting 24 hours before taking my first dose, but I was sure that he was lying. So, immediately after getting my prescription, I take my first dose of Suboxone. Now, I did not really know how it was supposed to make me feel, but I was fairly certain that this was not it. I felt like I had been feeling all morning, except now I was dizzy, and my body was tingly. The doctor told me that if I did not feel better after about twenty minutes, to take another one. He called it "loading up." So, I waited for the twenty minutes and took another one, which actually made me feel even worse. I was feeling the same symptoms, but now they were intensified. Maybe the doctor was right after all. Perhaps I should have waited for 24 hours before taking the medication. Either way, I got what I wanted. I was able to tell my parents, "See, I told you this wouldn't work!"

Once we returned home, I felt even worse. I desperately wanted to get high, but my parents took the keys to the car, and I had no money. All I could do was lie in bed and send out a bunch of text messages to people who I knew used drugs. I just laid there, hoping that something would happen. Nothing. But, just as I began to give up hope, a guy that I used to work with texted me back and informed me that he was no longer using heroin. He was now buying Suboxone off of the street.

"Yeah, man, I just got back from the Suboxone doc, but the shit ain't helping," I told him.

"How many you got? Wanna sell any?" He asked.

"I've got 87 of them left. I mean, they aren't helping me any, so yeah. How much do they go for?"

"I usually pay $15 apiece for them, but you can get up to $20 apiece sometimes," he said.

I struck gold, and suddenly, the hopeless feeling that I had just moments earlier was gone.

"Man, if you can come pick me up and take me to Cincinnati, I'll sell you as many as you want."

Within about thirty minutes, he was at my house. I sold him what he wanted and he gave me a good amount of money for them. He did not really want to take me to Cincinnati, but all I had to do was give him a free one and he agreed.

I somehow managed to find the perfect setup to fuel my addiction once again. Who knew that Suboxone could be worth so much money and that there was actually a market for it! I sure did not! But, it was a huge relief. It turned out that there was a pretty big market for them, actually. I was getting 90 per month with the potential of selling them for $20 apiece. That comes out to be $1,800 of profit straight into my pocket! Well, my veins. Not so much my pocket. My parents thought that I was taking my Suboxone, and that was why I appeared "normal." So, I took full advantage of the situation. They saw just how great I was doing, so they gave me the car back and began to trust me a little bit. I even started to pick up some shifts at my old job again. The only thing that I was worried about was my parents counting my prescription. Luckily, they never did. I had the perfect business and I intended to run it for the foreseeable future. My supply was good. The demand was great. It was consistent and gave me a 100% profit. It was a junkie's dream.

You can probably guess what happens next. All good things must come to an end, right? It was an end that I did not think of or plan for at all. My plan was to continue to sell my medication for months, or maybe even a couple of years. But, two things happened, neither of which I was ready for. One, my supply ran out early. My prescription was for me to take three per day. The problem was that I was selling anywhere between three and eight a day. It did not even dawn on me that this was going to cause me to go a week or two with no business or income. I was so focused on getting as much money as possible and spending it on heroin that I did not even think of the future (I never did if you have not noticed that by now). Not even a little bit. Then to the second issue. On October 6, 2013, I sold my last couple of Suboxone to a girl that I worked with. That particular morning, she and I both had to be at work at 11:00 a.m., so we met up early. She bought the last three Suboxone from me, so I had some money, then we headed across the river to Cincinnati to get some dope. She still used heroin. She just bought the Suboxone for emergencies. After meeting up with my dope boy, we drove back over to Kentucky. Normally, I would wait until I got home or got to work before I would shoot up. This time, I was feeling a little bit sick and anxious. I took my last shot before bed the night before, so it had been around twelve hours since my last use. I was withdrawing, and I was not willing to wait until we got to work to get the dope into my system. I decided to pull off of the Newport/Bellevue exit and proceeded to the Kroger parking lot. I had gotten high in that particular parking lot many times before. It was a busy place, which was good so that we would not be singled out like we would in an empty lot. There were also some bushes in the back of the lot to provide some cover. She, on the other hand, was much more patient than I. She asked me a couple of times to just go straight to work where it would be safe. To me, that was a completely unrealistic suggestion. I should have listened, but instead, I pulled into a parking spot. I was in a hurry because I wanted to feel better, and we were going to be late for work, so I prepped my needle, slid it into my arm, and pressed down on the plunger. The familiar sting. The blanket of warmth covering my body. The relief. I slowly glance over at her to see her struggling to find her vein. Then I glance to my left, out of the window, and as fast as the warm blanket came over me, it was removed. To my left, there was a Newport police officer walking straight toward us, holding eye contact with me the entire time.

"Alright. Stop what you are doing and get out of the car. Where is the rest of it?" the officer said calmly.

The tone of the officer's voice sounded like he had dealt with heroin addicts plenty of times before. He was not mad. He was not shocked or surprised. He seemed like it was just another typical day for him. It is pretty sad if you think about it.

I felt defeated. Helpless. "It's in my sock. There's a needle and a spoon," I replied.

There was no sense in trying to talk my way out of this one. I mean, the girl in my passenger seat still had everything sitting in her lap. Her arm bleeding all over my car did not help either.

"I was watching you for the last few minutes. Not too smart."

"Well, thanks for letting me finish my shot first," I said.

At least he let me get high before he decided to move in and arrest us. Nice guy!

As we were talking, three more police cruisers pulled up. We were then handcuffed, placed into the back of one of the cars, and sent to the police station. From there, we were separated into different holding cells, where we waited for about an hour. The entire time, I could not stop thinking. My mind was racing, and regret and fear were hitting me hard. My family. My kids. At that moment, I felt like I would never see them again. Throughout my drug use, I lied to my parents and stole everything from them. I fought with them about everything, used them, and took them for granted. But at that moment, I desperately wanted to hug them. It was a terrible feeling.

Once we were finished playing the waiting game at the police station, we were then moved to the Campbell County Detention Center. After an unnecessary strip search and booking process, we were left to wait some more in the booking room. Just waiting, for anything. Hours went by, and nothing. The way that I had dealt with jail in the past was to sleep as much as I possibly could, so that is what I did. I curled myself into a ball in the corner of the freezing cold stone and steel room and fell asleep. Who knows how much time had gone by, but I was soon awakened by one of the corrections officers.

"Mr. Peterson! Time to go to the big house!" he said.

I assumed that "big house" meant the courthouse. In jail, you have no idea what time it is. There were no windows, so I did not know if it was day or night. I just assumed that it was the next morning and that I was on my way to court to see the judge. But instead, they were actually referring to my house as the "big house." I was being released(O.R.'d). I was informed later that the jail was too overcrowded for minor drug charges. I was baffled as to how or why was being released, but I did not question their decision, nor did I ponder on it for too long. It was around 2:00 a.m., which meant that it had been about fifteen hours since my last shot. My mind was only focused on getting some money, finding a ride, and getting high.

I signed the necessary release papers, received my property, and walked straight out of the back door. First thing was first. I needed to call Alicia to come and pick me up. Second, think of a way to get some money from her. Third, somehow manage to talk her into taking me to Cincinnati so I could get some heroin. The phone only rang a couple of times, but of course, she answered. And of course, the scolding commenced. I needed her to give me money and a ride, so I just kept my mouth shut and let her yell at me all she wanted. I took it on the chin like a champ. When she arrived to pick me up, she was still yelling at me over the phone, but once I got into her car, I immediately blamed everything on the other girl. My story was that I was pulled over for speeding, but when the police officer ran our licenses, they decided to search the car and found a needle and heroin under the passenger seat. Since it was loose in my car and she did not claim it, I was charged with it. I thought it was a pretty good story. Up until then, my parents and Alicia thought that I was taking my prescription, so I still had that card to play. For step two, I told Alicia that the cops took my prescription, but I knew a guy in Ohio that sold Suboxone. As expected, she said no without even thinking about it, but persistence pays off. I just kept asking and telling her just how important it was for me to continue taking my medicine. Finally, she said yes and gave me the money. So, I called my "Suboxone dealer" at 4:00 in the morning and headed his way. The funny thing was that Alicia noticed that my "Suboxone dealer" and my heroin dealer lived in the same house. The gig was up. Everyone would now know that I was back to using heroin. Honestly, I really could not have cared less.

    Since I was released from jail with a drug charge, one of the terms of my release was that I take random drug tests until my court appearance. Clearly, there was no possible way that I was going to pass a drug screen. Over the course of my drug use, I had been experiencing chest pains for reasons unknown. The morning that I was called in for my drug screen, I had to rely on my chest pain as a way to get out of it. So, after I got the call, I went to the bathroom and used the end of my cell phone to put a big knot on my forehead. I literally hit my head over and over with the corner of my phone until it began to swell. I covered the knot with a hat and went back into the living room, complaining about my chest pain. Once I was left alone in the living room, I quietly stood up and hit the side of the piano with my hand to make a loud noise. After that, I quickly fell to the floor to make it appear that I had collapsed, hitting the piano with my head on the way down. I thought it was pretty genius, honestly. It was a better option than going in to fail a drug test and getting sent to jail again.

My parents took me to the hospital, which is exactly what I wanted to happen. The only way that I was going to be able to get out of the drug test was by having proof that I was in the hospital, so it worked out perfectly. I waited there for as long as they would let me. Then they discharged me and referred me to go see a specialist. I had seen other doctors about my chest pain in the past, but this time I felt really disrespected. The doctor, after examining me and asking me a number of questions, determined that the source of my chest pain was heartburn. He thought I was experiencing heartburn! The doctor wrote me a prescription and told me to take some heartburn medication, as well. What I actually heard him say was, "Ask your parents for $40. Doctor's orders."

That is exactly what I did. With the prescription in one hand and a note from the doctor suggesting that I take an over-the-counter medicine as well, I was easily able to get the money. The tricky part was since I was going to be spending the money on heroin, I was going to need proof that I got the medicine and spent the money on what it was intended for. There was nothing I could do about the prescription really, but I could still get the over-the-counter meds. All I had to do was steal them. I had stolen plenty of times before this, so it was nothing new to me. First thing was first, though; I had to get my dope.

Once I felt better and got to the grocery store, I casually walked inside so that I could scope things out. The store was not busy at all, which was going to make shoplifting more difficult. That meant that all eyes were going to be on me. All I could do was hope that nobody was watching the cameras. But, I had a mission to accomplish, and after doing some recon, I strolled on over to the pharmacy area and grabbed a box of heartburn medicine. It was not my style to just grab and go, so I headed over to the magazine section, picked one up, and pretended to read. I took my time to calm my nerves. Then I glance up to see an employee stocking the shelves in the aisle that I was in. Her back was facing me. Now was my chance. I stood up and stuck the box inside the waistline of my pants and began to walk toward the front doors. I kept my eyes forward. The doors opened. I took exactly one step past the door when I felt a tight grasp on my left arm, followed by a badge in my face and a voice stating, "Don't resist me. Come on."

All I thought was "shit..." Every step toward the security office got worse than the last. The feeling that I felt at the police station just a couple of weeks ago came back. The same feeling of helplessness. The intense urge to hug my son and daughter (who had been born during this time) and parents. The feeling that I would never, ever see them again. How was I going to get out of this one? Well, I wasn't. Although I begged and pleaded uncontrollably with the security officer to let me go, he still called the police. I do not think that he heard a single thing that I was saying to him.

My last attempt was with the police officer. I mean, it was only a $10 item that I was attempting to steal. Were they really going to waste their time on taking me to jail for that? I doubt it. They would either have me pay for it or ban me from the store or both. But, there is no way that they would take me to jail. I had to play my cards right, though, so when the officer walked into the room, I slowly stood up and stuck my hand out to greet him. A sign of respect from me to him. "Don't shake my hand. Sit down!" Well played, Mr. Officer. Well played.

Those six words told me enough. I was screwed. Now I knew that I was definitely going to jail, which was the start of the worst withdrawal that I had ever experienced.

A Second, Second Chance

The next morning, my name was called for video court. This was court, but instead of going to the actual courthouse, I was taken to a small room where I spoke to the judge through a television screen. There were about twenty of us crammed into this room. One by one, we were called up to the screen to seal our fate. When my name was called, I walked up to the screen, informed of what I was being charged with, and then I was given my recommended sentence. "The prosecutor recommends ten days in jail. How do you plead?" The judge asked.

All I wanted to do was get the hell out of there, but the voices from the inmates behind me were saying, "Ten days!? I'd take that!" or something along those lines. Without even really thinking about it, I pled guilty and immediately regretted it. Ten days is not a long time, but to a hardcore heroin addict like me, it was a lifetime.

Since I was now officially "final sentenced," I was taken to the Class D dorm. This dorm was the one that housed all of the inmates who had also been final sentenced. The inmates in Class D were assigned jobs which helped pass the time and allowed them to make a little bit of money. The money could then be used to buy phone cards, food, clothing, or other items from commissary. It was very uncommon for an inmate to be final sentenced in just one day like I was. My point is that I was the only inmate in the entire dorm who was detoxing from heroin, or any substance for that matter. Hoping for some sympathy, I received anger and frustration from the other inmates. This only made me feel worse. I was in a dorm with 71 other inmates, but I felt completely alone. There was one man who gave me a good suggestion, though. He said that anytime he had to go through withdrawal in jail, he would spend as much time in the shower as he could. So, I tried that, but it did not help me at all. The standing hurt too much. All I could do was lay in my rack. Even then, there were no pillows, and we were not allowed under the blankets from 5:00 a.m. to 4:30 p.m. Man, it was miserable.

On day three of my detox, which was the worst day, I realized that I had not eaten or drunk anything since before I was arrested. That night, I tried to drink some water. It was hard to swallow, but I forced it down in hopes that having something in my stomach would help. When I laid back down in my rack, I almost immediately threw up. Just liquid, everywhere. It was all over my blanket and sheet and on the wall next to me, which then ran down to the floor. I was far too embarrassed and felt way too bad to do anything about it. It was late at night and I was fairly certain that everyone else was sleeping, so I just rolled over to the very edge of my rack and closed my eyes like nothing had even happened. Conveniently, the next morning at 5:00 a.m., we had a shakedown/dorm inspection/harassment session. I was trying the shower trick again when I heard, "Peterson! Peterson!"

I acknowledged the officer that I heard him and got out of the shower as quickly as I could. By the time I made my way over to the officer, my vomit-covered blanket, sheet, and mattress were all on the floor in the middle of a circle of inmates. That may have been one of the most embarrassing moments of my life. For an entire hour, the officer made me stay on the ground cleaning my mattress. Dope sick and being judged and laughed at by the other inmates, it was rough, to say the least.

After that monumental moment of my life, I began to feel a little bit better each day. I was slowly able to eat some food and keep water down. I started by eating just one slice of bread a day. Then two. Then after a week or so, I was able to eat a whole tray. The trays were ridiculously small, but my point is that I was getting better. Following that, I started to socialize with the other inmates. There was a lot of card playing and a lot of time watching television. But, it felt good to be able to get out of bed to do it. Mentally, I was able to think more clearly. Mainly guilty thoughts about my past year of using heroin and lies. I did a lot of reflecting. And then it hit me. I had a thought, "Matt, you've been given another chance to get clean. Another chance at life. Do not fuck this up!"

Maybe it was me telling myself that. But looking back at that moment, today, I believe that it was most certainly God who said it.

He had never spoken to me that clearly before, but I have been drug-free ever since.

My jail journey was not over yet, though. I was busted for shoplifting in Kenton County, but I was now on a hold for Campbell County. Since I was out on bond in Campbell County for the possession charge a few weeks prior, this shoplifting charge caused my bond to be revoked. My sentence for the shoplifting charge was ten days in Kenton County Detention Center. On day thirteen, I was shipped over to Campbell County jail, where I would stay for the next month. I was held in "the back pods" for the first ten days. The pods were the part of the jail that had smaller cells. It was made up of a big, circular room with two floors. On each floor, there were six cells which held ten inmates each. My cell had thirteen, meaning that three of us were sleeping on the floor. The only thing that we had to do was talk, eat, or play cards. I became a professional Spades player while I was in there.

Finally, during my court appearance, I get some good news. Since I was a father, and still technically had my job at the restaurant, the judge allowed me to have work release. This meant that I would be able to leave the jail, go to work, then return back to the jail after my shift was over. Basically, I would just be sleeping at the jail. Also, being on work release, I was sent across the parking lot to a separate building. Just like Kenton County, it was the Class D facility. The difference between the two was insane! I was able to wear my own clothes, have my MP3 player and even have my own shaver! It did not feel like jail at all. The building was made up of two dorm rooms holding about fifty people in each one. Each dorm was equipped with a flat-screen television, four private showers, and a small recreational yard that we had access to all day. On the recreational yard, there were some picnic tables and cornhole boards set up. Morale over there was fairly high most of the time because of how laid back it was. This made it easy to make "friends," but I still had to be careful. Jail politics are nothing to joke around about. Most of the other inmates were given work by the county. While they were out working, they would have people that they knew bring them tobacco and drugs that they would then sneak back into the jail. Even in jail, I was tempted with drugs almost on a daily basis. Surprisingly, I did not have any problem at all turning them down. I remembered that moment of clarity that I had in the Kenton County Jail.

    I had not yet been final sentenced, so I had no idea how long I was going to be in jail this time. Little did I know, but my parents had been working on getting me bonded out. It was close to Christmas time, and I had a newborn baby girl named Myla. Nobody wanted me to have to miss out on her first Christmas. No matter how much pain I had caused my family, they understood that missing Myla's first Christmas was a time that I would never get back, and it was important to everyone that I was there to experience it. My bond was set at $2,500, and since I had stolen everything from my family, they used the only thing that they had left to give. They used their house as my bond. I could not believe that they would do that for me, but on December 23, 2013, I was bonded out of jail and on my way home to spend the holidays with my family.

That Christmas was extra special to me for a number of reasons. One, this was the first Christmas in a very long time that I was not worried about getting the receipts from my parents. For the past few years, I had always taken all of my presents back to the stores. Not because I did not like the gifts, but because I needed the cash more. Two, I was able to put together the toys for my kids. Instead of being focused on myself or how I was going to sneak away so that I could get high, I, for the first time in years, was able to be completely present. The greatest gift that I was given that year was not a present. It was not even done intentionally. When it was time to eat, the rest of the family went into the dining room while I stayed in the family room to finish putting together a toy. I was alone. As I glanced over, there, within an arms reach of me, was my mother's purse. This may sound silly to you, but to me, this was a huge deal. I had stolen money out of that same purse so many times that my mother would have to keep her purse with her at all times. Toward the end of my career as a professional drug addict, my behavior even caused her to sleep with her purse in bed with her.

That did not stop me. I would wait until they were asleep and then I would army crawl up the stairs and into her room. As quietly as possible, I would stand up to reach over her and slowly take as much cash out of her purse as I could before returning back downstairs to call my dope boy. Now here I am, on Christmas day in a room alone with that same purse. She trusted me. That was the best gift I have ever gotten.

I enjoyed my time out on bond. I was still required to take random drug screens just like last time. The difference this time, though, was that I did not have to fake chest pains or hit myself in the head repeatedly with a cell phone to con my way out of it. I went willingly and passed every one of them. My bond, however, was only to keep me out of jail until my last court appearance where I was to be final sentenced. I did my best not to worry about what the sentence would be. The prosecutor recommended that I spend the next year in jail. My attorney and friends from my support group all told me that I would probably just get probation since I had been out on bond for the last three months with no slip-ups. The drug screen results would also be used in my favor. So, on March 18, 2014, I went to the courthouse to find out what the Department of Corrections had in store for me. I went into the courtroom with confidence and with high hopes.

"Sixty more days in jail and three years of supervised probation."

Well, that seemed a bit harsh if you ask me.

The judge gave me one week to turn myself in so I could begin my sixty days in jail. The good news, though, was that he allowed me to remain on work release. I was thankful for the work release because I had just gotten a new job at Bonefish Grille in Crescent Springs, Kentucky, and I was scheduled to start on the 23rd of March. Just two days before I had to turn myself in.

On March 25th, I headed back to jail. This time was not nearly as bad as my past experiences, however. I had never been to jail sober before, so going in without the fear and anxiety of withdrawal was nice. Also, most of the inmates that I met a few months earlier were still there. Knowing most of the inmates made my time a lot easier. I still had to face drug use while I was in there, but the other guys were respectful of my decision to remain sober. I would still buy up all of the cigarettes that I could get, though. Especially on Fridays. For one, nobody went out to work on the weekends, which meant that I had to make sure that I bought as many as I could to make sure that I would have enough to last me until Monday. Also, the Campbell County Jail was directly across the Ohio River from the Cincinnati Reds stadium, The Great American Ballpark. Every Friday home game that they had would end with a ten-minute firework show. During those ten minutes out on the recreational yard, I was free. The cage that enclosed the yard, the corrections officers, the jail, the inmates, my past, it all disappeared.

Those sixty days in jail were my last. I figured out that if you do not break the law, you do not go to jail. Weird... But, I still had a lot of growing up and adjusting to do. I was out of jail, but I was still on probation for the next three years. Being on probation was stressful, but it also really helped me. I needed that extra little bit of accountability. It was motivation for me to stay clean, for if I relapsed, I would go back to jail. Probation also required me to have a full-time job or be in college, which kept me focused on being a productive member of society. Something that I had not been for over a decade. Or maybe ever? But this accountability kept me engaged at Bonefish as a line cook. I loved to cook, and I was good at it. Just after a few months, I was promoted to Assistant Culinary Manager. Holding this title gave me the responsibility of opening the store in the mornings. I was a heroin addict for so long, and now here I am being trusted with the keys and security code to a four-star restaurant! That was a blessing in itself, but there was another blessing lurking around. A server. Her name was Megan. I remember the first time that I saw her through the expo window. When I saw her, I nudged the cook next to me and said, "Bro, who the hell is that?"

He replied with, "Her? Oh, that's Megan. She's taken, though, so don't even waste your time."

That was a hard pill to swallow, but little did I know, she was on the other side of the expo window asking another server about me. "Hey, who is the new cook?"

I did not pursue her because I was under the assumption that she was in a relationship, but then I found out the truth. One of my other line cooks informed me that she had not been in a relationship for about a month. So, I made my move. One night after our dinner rush, she ordered herself some food. A spinach salad with salmon. No butter or seasoning on the salmon. Dressing on the side. She also put a note on the bottom of the ticket, which read, "No Stems." For the next forty minutes or so, I cooked her the most beautiful salmon that you can imagine and hand-picked off every single stem from every single piece of spinach. Well, needless to say, it worked, and the rest is history. We ended up dating and moving in to a small apartment together within just a few months. Yeah... my cooking is that good.

During this time, we were both going through some major changes in our lives. I was still newly sober and had no real direction for my life. She had recently graduated from the University of Cincinnati and had a dream of starting her own business. She had a direction for her life, and one day she asked me "Are you just going to work in a restaurant for the rest of your life? You have so much more that you can offer the world. What do you want to do?"

Up to that point, I had never really thought about it. When drugs were running my life, I did not have to worry about a career or a direction that I wanted my life to go. I was convinced that I was going to die as a heroin addict, so, no point in planning for the future. Even after getting clean, I still carried around a lot of guilt. I had low self-esteem and zero confidence. My view of myself was that I was still a low life drug addict with nothing to offer anyone. But, when she asked me that question, I realized that my future was here. I was not dead. I was not a heroin addict any longer. I had worth. I had potential. The problem was that I had spent so long doing drugs that I was not good at anything. I was a good cook, but I was not willing to work in a kitchen forever. Then, all of a sudden, it hit me. "I'm really good with drugs!"

The heroin epidemic was booming, and I had a ton of experience with it. I began to look up different colleges and programs for drug addiction and I came across a program at Cincinnati State Technical and Community College. They had a two-year program to become and addiction counselor. This was it! For over half of my life, I had been training for my future and did not even know it. In the summer of 2015, I enrolled at Cincinnati State. In the Spring of 2017, I graduated with my Associate of Arts degree, my Addiction Counseling certificate and I also obtained my Chemical Dependency Counselor's Assistant (CDCA) license through the state of Ohio.

My journey did not end there however. Immediately after graduating from Cincinnati State, I enrolled as a student at Northern Kentucky University to pursue my bachelor's degree in Psychology. My master's degree may even be in the picture.

I now had my direction. I found my purpose for my life and I continue to build. Megan followed her dream, as well. She already had a degree from UC, but she took it even further and get a license to become a personal trainer. Her education, certification, passion and determination all came together one day, and her business was born. M_Pire. She did it. She made her dream into a reality and has been walking that path ever since. She was even training me. I used to be athletic back in the day, and I wanted to get back into shape. She taught me how to eat healthy and wrote me workout programs that would benefit me the best. It was not too hard considering I lived with a fitness instructor! Above all, she taught me how to love myself. I will tell you though, getting back into shape helped me out tremendously! As I mentioned, my drug use stripped me of all confidence and self-esteem that I had. Lifting weights, getting physically fit, and creating new friendships with people who shared the same passion for fitness not only helped me physically, but mentally, as well. I began to feel good about myself. I felt in control. If there was something that I did not like about myself, I knew that I had the power to change it. Heroin was no longer in charge. I called the shots, and it was an incredible feeling to finally know that!

Although I was growing as a person and my life was becoming what I could have never imagined, Megan still insisted that I go to AA meetings. I would go, but I found myself trying to get her to go with me. We did not fight very often, but when we did, it was normally about alcohol. Megan drank. I did not. Deep down, I wanted to drink, but I could not. I was still on probation. If I drank, I would have been taking a chance of going back to jail. Also, my sobriety was important to me, and it included not drinking. Since I could not drink, I did not want her to drink either. She had told me stories from when she was in college about how she and her friends would drink and about some of the crazy things they would do. I used her stories to try and convince her that she had a drinking problem and needed to stop. At the time, I thought that I was doing her a favor. Looking back on it now, I was being 100% selfish. I just did not want her to drink because I couldn't.

Testing My Sobriety

Now, I never won too many arguments with her. I still don't actually, but I started to win this one and she began to go to the Big A meeting with me on Wednesday nights. I was so happy to be able to share sobriety with her. The other upside to her attending meetings was that it was also good publicity for her business. I knew a lot of people from being in recovery off and on for a couple of years. A lot of them had seen her fitness videos that she would post on social media and also saw the progress that I was making. I was proud to introduce her to everyone who showed interest in getting into shape. We were partners and I wanted to help her grow her business. It was great. Friends, fitness, sobriety and my girlfriend. Nothing bad could possibly come from this.

    Unfortunately, sobriety is not all sunshine and rainbows. The more Megan came to the Big A with me, the more people she met in hopes of growing her business. Which was great. But, one night I introduced her to a man that I had seen around but did not know well. He expressed interest to me about getting into shape and asked me what I was doing. I gave all of the credit to Megan and set the two of them up. Everything was fine at first. She did not have her own gym to work out of yet, so she would go to his house to train him for an hour on the same night of every week, just like all of her other clients. She would always get home around 9:30 or at least close to it, and she would always text me when she was on her way home. One night, she did not, so I texted her, with no response. Then I called her. No answer. Finally, she texted me back and said that she was just talking to him about some things and that she would be home a little late. 11:00 p.m. and she still was not home, so, pissed off, I decided to just go on to bed. When she finally came home at 1:30 in the morning, I knew what was going on.

    From that night, our relationship began to slowly fall apart. We were arguing more. We were tense around each other. Our nightly routines began to fade out, and eventually, she admitted to me that she did not know if she wanted to be with me anymore. I did my best to try to change her mind, but within just a couple of days, she finally told me that she really liked the other guy that I introduced her to at the Big A not long ago. She told me that she was not ready for a "married lifestyle" and that she wanted to have more fun. I was ready to settle down, she, on the other hand, wanted to party and hop on the back of this guy's motorcycle. I begged with her not to leave me, but after an hour or two, I realized that there was nothing that I could say or do that was going to change her mind. So, I walked back to our bedroom and grabbed the engagement ring that I had for her out of our closet where I hid it. I threw the ring one her lap and said, "Just so you know, this is where my heart is!"

The rest of it is just a big blur of crying, yelling, cursing and wall punches. I returned to the bedroom and threw my clothes into a couple of garbage bags, got into my car and drove straight to the nearest bar. I was completely heartbroken and baffled as to how this all happened. As I sat in the bar parking lot, I just thought. Should I go in? How could she do this to me? I was trying to help her and her business. I was trying to help him and his fitness. I was the one who introduced them to each other at an A.A. meeting. My A.A. meeting, where I felt the safest! I blamed her. I blamed him. I blamed Alcoholics Anonymous. I blamed God.

I never did go into that bar. Instead, I just sat there and cried. Once I felt that I was able to take a break from the tears, I called my old friend Kyle. He was living in a sober living home during this time and I now had nowhere to live. Luckily for me, his roommate had just moved out of the sober living home, so I moved in with him. Once I arrived, Kyle helped me unload my car while I brought him up to speed about everything that had just happened. From that point on, Kyle seemed to have put his life on hold for me. Just to keep me company and to make sure that I did not do anything stupid that I was going to regret. All I wanted to do was get high or drunk, or both, but he cared enough about me to make sure that I stayed sober. Since Megan and I worked together, I quit my job, which gave Kyle plenty of work to do. I had nothing to do at all, but I did not care.

Throughout the next couple of months, Kyle rarely left my side. He did have to return to work, but if he was not at work, he was with me. I cannot count how many times he broke plans with other people for me. Or how many times that he went into work late or took off early because I was struggling. We were best friends and he single-handedly got me through until I was able to get back on my feet. Over time, I slowly began to glue the pieces of my heart back together. I got a new job and really started to put my focus back onto school and my physical fitness. My new job was even at a new gym that had just opened up. The gym helped me out a lot. It was like an escape from life for me. In the past, I would use drugs and alcohol as my escape, but now, I turned to a healthier option. For about two hours, every single day, I would throw my headphones in my ears to shut off the noise of the world, and I would lift weights. Due to everything that had taken place at the Big A, I started to shy away from Alcoholics Anonymous. That place was my sanctuary, but I was betrayed. I resented A.A. and most of the people in it because of what happened. So, the gym became my recovery. Kyle helped me emotionally. College helped me mentally. The gym helped me emotionally, mentally and physically.

It was not that I did not need Kyle anymore, but once I started to get my mind straight again, we began to live our own separate lives. We were both working full time and I was in school. Any free time that I had, I spent working out at the gym. We still lived together, though, so we would hang out in the evenings on most nights. Normally, we would just put on a funny movie and laugh as much as possible. Other nights, he would invite his girlfriend over and the three of us would talk and laugh and just have a good time. Sometimes we would go out and grab some food. We had a good routine going on for a while. Then Kyle started to stay out all night at his girlfriend's place, so I thought.

At some point, Kyle started to become distant. He seemed like he was troubled by something when I saw him, which was not very often anymore. Something just was not adding up, but I tried not to put too much thought into it. Then, one night, he told me that he was going to go stay at his girlfriend's house. This was not out of the ordinary. What was out of the ordinary, though, was that his girlfriend called me later that same night and asked me if I had seen Kyle. Apparently, Kyle told her that he was going to be hanging out with me. This was alarming to both of us, for he lied to the two people who cared about him the most. She then informed me that he had not been going to work and that they had been arguing a lot. After we got off of the phone with each other, I immediately called him to make sure that he was alright. No luck. I did not hear back from him at all that night. I was worried about him, but he had always had a very independent, "nobody can control me" type of attitude. Maybe he was just being Kyle?

I brushed off that night and convinced myself that he was fine, but his behavior continued over the next few days and I began to wonder if he was getting high again. Then one afternoon he called me and said that he was on his way back to the house and asked me if I wanted to go out and grab something to eat before I went to work. When he arrived at the house, I got in his van with him and he drove up the road to a pizza place. We ate in his van, along with an elephant. It was obvious that I was worried about him. It was also obvious that he had something that he needed to get off of his chest, and without having to do any digging at all, he opened up. For the first time ever, he was honest with me about relapsing. I remember our conversation very well. He told me that there was a guy that he worked with that got a prescription of Percocet and asked Kyle to sell them for him. Against his better judgement, Kyle agreed to sell the pills for him, but he ended up swallowing them instead. Then he followed up by telling me that he only lasted a couple of days before he ended back up on heroin.

"Matt, I don't want to do this again. I don't want to go back to the way I was."

For the first time in the history of our friendship, I witnessed him crying. He begged me not to go to work that night.

"I don't want to be alone. I'm afraid of what I'll do."

I had work, though, so I told him to hang tight and that I would be back.

That was the last conversation that I ever had with Kyle W. Ossege. Two days went by with no contact at all. His friends and his family were all calling me, trying to figure out where he was. Nobody could find him. Finally, I had no choice but to call Chris, the owner of the sober living house, and tell him that Kyle has been missing and owes rent. Chris responded with, "I saw his van parked at Walmart around noon today. I'll swing back by there and see if he is still there. Maybe he is living in his van."

"I'll meet you there," I said.

I was in no way prepared for what I was about to find.

After the coroner finished at the scene, I then went to Kyle's father and step-mother's house to inform them. It was around 11:00 p.m. when his parents finally woke up to me banging on their window. After they answered the door and let me in, his father sat down and waited for me to say something. I could not get a single word out of my mouth. Finally, he had to ask me.

"He's not gone, is he?" He asked

"Yeah, bro," I replied.

Those are the only two words that I could get out before falling to my knees at his father's feet.

The next couple of weeks were just a blur, but I did not have much down time after he passed away. I spent a lot of time supporting his friends and talking to his family. He was loved by a lot of people. I was struck by guilt. Kyle put his life on hold as much as he could for me. To keep me sober. To keep me company. He did everything that he could for me when I needed him. He is the reason why I did not relapse during that time in my life. But, I did not return the favor, and I still, to this day, have not fully forgiven myself for it.

Eventually I had to start to move forward with my life. The only thing that I could think of doing was to really focus on school and to hit the gym harder than ever. I also started to post some motivational videos on social media. Both college and working out helped my confidence and my self-esteem a lot. The loss of Kyle became my primary source of motivation. Those three things together put me on a path of transformation into a new person. I became very caring toward other people, especially addicts. I had a new confidence level like I had never experienced before. I felt good about myself. I found a path and I quickly began to fall into my purpose for still being alive.

My life was going better than it ever had. It was a very strange feeling for me, an ex-heroin addict, to have. Then, one night while I was at the gym, my life got a little bit more interesting. I received an email. I get emails all of the time, but this one was different. This one was from my ex-girlfriend, Megan. The email was annoyingly long and made my heartrate increase with every line. Apparently, she missed me and thought about me all of the time. It had been close to ten months since we had split up. I tried not to respond, but the longer I worked out, the more I thought about the email. Then I realized something. When she broke my heart those ten months ago, she must have kept a piece of it. I ended up emailing her back before I left the gym that night.

Within just a couple of days, we ended up having a very romantic dinner together at McDonald's. Leading up to our meeting, I felt excited, but very nervous. What helped me the most was knowing that I had leverage since she was the one who left me. I felt like that would give me some control over the conversation. Yet, I really had no clue how our meeting was going to go.

    The beginning went well, and I held my ground. I kept my head held high and did my best to show no weakness or signs of attraction to her. Throughout our conversation, I made sure that she knew just how well I was doing and that I was just fine without her. On the outside, I was putting on a great show. On the inside, however, I knew that I missed her, and by the time that we said our goodbyes for the evening, I felt myself falling back in love with her. Trust me, I did my very best to fight it, but the feeling proved itself to be too intense to control. We emailed back and fourth for a few weeks. Yes, you read this correctly. Email. She was technically still with the other guy and she felt like emailing was "more professional". But whatever. I just went along with it. It was good to be talking to her again.

    Over the next few weeks, we just kept getting closer and closer. We had a lot of great talks, strong laughs and even a couple of dates, which were referred to as "business meetings". Our time together was very enjoyable, but I still carried a lot of resentment toward her and what she did to me. This resentment came out when I finally had to give her a choice. Him, or me? It was undeniable, even after what she did to me and all of the time had passed, that she still held my heart. I did a lot of growing over the last ten months. Growing that I would not have been able to do if we had stayed together. This made it easier for me to forgive her. But, we had now reached a point where I just could not wait any longer. She had to choose.

The short version is, she chose to stay with him, and since I was completely unwilling to merely be friends, I decided that we needed to cut ties altogether. The good news to the story is that she only ended up staying with him for another couple of weeks, and when she reached out to me, I jumped at the opportunity. She did say that she wanted to remain "single" until the fall time, but during that time, we did everything that a couple would do. Then, when fall finally arrived, we made it official.

Blessings Of Sobriety

One of Megan's favorite things to do is run. She would run for fun a lot, but she also ran in races ranging from 5K to a full marathon (26.2 miles). Now, I am not a runner. The thought of running "for fun" completely baffles me. But at the same time, I knew that running was one of her favorite activities, and I wanted to do as many things with her as I could. Having said that, I agreed to run in the Thanksgiving Day Race with her that year. This was a big race for me. For us both really. This was the first race that I had ever been in. The course was 6.2 miles long, and for me, it was a very awkward run. Here is why. In our previous relationship, I wanted to marry her. Well, that feeling carried over into our new relationship. Even after all that we had gone through together, I had no doubt, zero, that she was the one that I wanted to walk, or run, through life with. In the weeks leading up to the race, I was saving money for the perfect engagement ring. A white gold, rose-shaped ring with a single diamond in the center, which I paid off and picked up just a couple of days before the race. Since it was Thanksgiving, my first race, our first race together, and being one of her favorite things to do, I decided that this would be the perfect time to propose. The reason that it was an awkward run for me was that, for 6.2 miles, I ran with my hands in my pockets to keep a grasp on the ring so it did not go flying out into the street.

After crossing the finish line, I gathered the other four people that we ran the race with and asked each of them to say something that they are thankful for. I went last. "I'm thankful for all of you and my family." I then turned toward Megan and took her by the hand. "I'm also thankful for you. I love you and I love doing these kinds of things with you."

Right then, she interrupted me and said, "Matt, you're being weird. It was just a 6-mile race..."

I brushed it off and continued. "I want to do these types of things with you for the rest of my life," and as I lowered myself down to one knee, I asked, "Will you marry me?"

I waited, down on one knee, in front of hundreds of people at the finish line, waiting for her to answer me. She never did answer me. She just stood there and cried, then laughed, then cried some more. But, she took the ring and allowed me to put it on her finger, so I took that as a yes.

The good life did not stop there. Just a couple of months after we became engaged, we found out that we were going to have our first child together. On Halloween of 2017, Marley Joy Peterson was born, and my world was complete.

As I had mentioned, I spent a long time blaming God for the life that he had given me. However, after I had gotten clean and my outlook on life began to change, I realized that I had just been living the life that He had planned out for me all along. As I looked back over my life as a drug addict, I could find countless times where I should have died, but God kept showing up, time after time. Even when He was not invited, He was still there, carrying me through everything. I realized that this was a relationship that I was not going to turn my back on. Throughout my drug use, I viewed myself as a victim. Nothing was my fault, everyone had it out to get me, the court system is crooked, and God hated me. Now that I have some sense, I can see that God was just prepping me for my career all along.

    I have had a couple of different jobs since I've been clean. I never returned to Bonefish. Instead, I worked at a gym, and at a furniture store which was owned by a good friend of mine. Then, as I was scrolling through Facebook, I came across a post that mentioned a job opening at the Grateful Life Center, the same treatment facility that saved my life. There was God, showing off again! The position was to become the food service supervisor, which meant that I would be in charge of creating menus and making sure that 350 clients were fed properly. I was offered the job, and after holding that position for a few months, another position opened up, and I became one of the case managers. It was a very rewarding job for me to have, and it was responsible for jumpstarting me into my career.

I stayed with the Grateful Life Center for a little over a year before I was offered a position as a peer recovery specialist at Brightview Health in Ohio. My job there, if you can even call it a job, was to speak to, encourage, and help newly recovering addicts. I was able to use all of my worst experiences from my life as a tool to help other people. My life turned out to not be a waste after all! Around the same time, I became the chairman of a non-profit organization called People Advocating Recovery Northern Kentucky. The organization is a statewide non-profit based out of Louisville, Kentucky. I was asked to take over the Northern Kentucky chapter, which has given me one more way to help fight against addiction, and one more reason I know God is a beast! To take it even further, I am also a college graduate, a public speaker, and an author! I have four amazing children, Christian, Myla, Riley, and Marley, a fantastic, strong, smart and stunning partner, a home, my own car, a career, friends, and a life that just keeps getting better I do not say these things to toot my own horn or for recognition. I say these things because of where I came from. I say these things because I should not even be alive. I say these things because they are proof that there is life beyond addiction!

Thoughts of an Addict

This portion of the book is dedicated to my own thoughts and opinions about addiction. I will touch on some controversial topics. I will also go over some things that have helped me in my recovery, as well as things that have not. Some of what you read may upset or anger you. You may disagree with me when it comes to certain things. Perhaps you will be relieved to read what I have to say and agree with me in full. Or maybe you will not have an opinion on the matter but are simply reading this to gain more of an understanding. Regardless, these are answers and opinions that I have obtained over years of living the life of a drug addict, and my goal is to bring understanding and insight to you about this very misunderstood epidemic. Furthermore, I will give resources for support and treatment for both the addict and their loved ones, for I have found that the family and friends of the addict need just as much support.

Why Does the Using Start?

There are many different reasons why people begin to use drugs. Perhaps the most common reason comes from the social interaction with other people who use drugs or alcohol. Many young peopleexperiment with drugs and alcohol due to peer pressure or in an attempt to simply fit in. Just as I did, teenagers will have the thought that they will never be able to fit in or be considered one of the "cool kids" unless they partake in the party scene. Having been one of those teens myself, I can look back at my life and realize that there were two main reasons as to why I gave into peer pressure. One, I was not comfortable with myself at all. I had low self-esteem and absolutely zero confidence. Being an only child raised in a Christian home, I was completely sheltered from drugs, alcohol, and the type of people who I shared a neighborhood with. This brings me to reason number two. I was completely uneducated about drugs, addiction, and about the situation that I was putting myself into. My only knowledge regarding drugs came from the famous D.A.R.E. program that was around when I was in elementary school. This was a totally useless program, by the way. "Just say no?" Oh man, if it were only that easy! For one, if you are a young, lonely, sheltered, awkward kid with no self-esteem, it is a lot harder to "just say no" than one might think. You will be willing to do some pretty crazy things in order to obtain friends. And for two, I took part in the D.A.R.E. program when I was eight years old. Being that young, I was totally oblivious to what the police officer was talking about. I think it would be safe to say that most eight-year-old kids do not know what fentanyl or methamphetamine is. Obviously, yes, it is extremely important to speak with your children about drugs, and I want to encourage you to do so. In my opinion, I would say around ten or eleven years old would be a good age. Be open with your children. If you have experimented with substances, tell them that. If you feel like you are too uneducated on the subject, then educate yourself or find a specialist in your area for you and your family to meet with. If you are a parent, it is your duty to educate, prepare, and protect them!

Depression is another big reason why people begin to take various types of drugs. This is also something that I struggled with as I grew up, and let me tell you, nothing makes drugs and alcohol more appealing than feeling completely alone, worthless, and have nothing to live for. When I reached a point that my life felt unbearable, I thought to myself that the world would be better off without me. It became very difficult for me to find a reason not to use drugs. Many of my friends were using drugs, as well, but the difference was that they were using to enjoy life and to have a good time. I started off that way, but unlike them, I was fighting a demon inside of me that was trying to kill me. My friends had plans for their future. They had goals and a vision of where they wanted to be ten years down the road. I did not. I could not see that far into the future. That was a tough place for me to be. Stuck in place. Feeling hopeless. Obviously, getting ridiculously intoxicated is not the best way to pull yourself out of depression, but it is definitely the easier option.

Another reason that people begin to use drugs, and I hear this a lot, is because a doctor prescribed opiates to them. Before the heroin epidemic impacted our country, doctors had more of a freedom to prescribe pain killers to patients. Sometimes they were needed. Other times they were not. A lot of times, patients were over-medicated. As I mentioned in my story, I spent a couple of years "doctor shopping." Every time that I went to a new doctor, I would get more pain pills. I would get stronger pain pills. And it was very easy to do. Since then, doctors have been warned to be much more careful when it comes to prescribing pain medication.

Throughout my drug-using career, and now that I am clean, I can see almost exactly how this epidemic began. Through my eyes, I have watched hundreds, or thousands, of people that I know personally who ended up using heroin because they were first prescribed opiate pain killers. I can honestly say that I do not know a single heroin addict, clean or actively using, who went straight to heroin. Nearly all of them, myself included, started their heroin use because they met with a doctor. Now, I am not blaming the doctors.

I believe that most of us were simply uneducated when it came to the effects of opiates. I do not believe that it was anyone's intention to get millions of Americans hooked on opiates. I also want to note that there are plenty of people who need prescription opiates due to severe injury or disease. However, I do know of a certain pharmaceutical company that intentionally released marketing campaigns for their drug, Oxycontin. When it comes to prescription pain killers, Oxycontin was the "big dog" of them all. Being one of the most dangerous, powerful, and addictive pain meds on the market, it was advertised as 100% safe and non-addictive. Taking oxycontin as prescribed was dangerous enough, but this drug was often abused by being snorted or injected into the body with a needle, and once it was realized how dangerous oxycontin really was, it was reformulated into a pill that was no longer able to be crushed into powder. Oxycontin was the most powerful and enjoyable pain killer at the time, but using a pain killer that strong caused the user's tolerance to skyrocket. Once the pill was reformulated and no longer able to be crushed into a powder, addicts then began to turn to heroin, causing the market to explode. I cannot say if the pharmaceutical company did this on purpose or not (my opinion would be yes based on the fact that it was marketed as non-addictive and safe), but either way, this played a huge role in the jumpstart of the heroin epidemic.

Choice or Not?

Perhaps the most controversial subject of addiction, is it a choice or not? Being an addict, I have lived through and experienced an entirely different side of life that you probably have not. Have you ever lied in order to use drugs? Have you ever stolen anything from your loved ones to get high? Have you ever been homeless because your addiction has stripped you from everything? Unless you are an addict, then I would guess you answered no to those questions. I would also guess that you would not consider any of these things to be rational decisions. Well, you are right. During my drug use, these are just some of the things that I did because of my addiction. Those weren't even the worst. I did not want to do any of it, but I did nonetheless. I reached a point where I no longer had a choice in the matter. Opiates had such a firm grasp on me that I did not have any control over my decision making. I was conscious of what I was doing and that it was wrong, but I literally could not help myself. I had to do anything and everything to make sure that I got opiates into my system.

This is how I ended up, but as I look back at my drug use, I noticed that there was a process that I had to go through to get to where I ended up. When I was first introduced to pain killers when I was hit by the church van in seventh grade, I knew that I enjoyed the way that they made me feel. However, I did not think anything of it at the time, and when they were gone, they were gone. Simple as that. Then, I was reintroduced to them, years later, after I had my wisdom teeth cut out of my head. I still enjoyed the way that they made me feel. The difference was that this time, I was hanging out with a different group of people. People who enjoyed partying and using drugs on the occasion. This made them even more appealing to me, and I began to use them socially. Once I ran out of my prescription, I would buy them off of people that I knew from time to time. Then I sought them out every weekend. Then the weekends got longer. It went from Friday and Saturday, to Thursday through Saturday. Then to Thursday to Sunday. Then Wednesday to Sunday, until I was eventually doing them every day. The alarming thing about all of this was that I was 100% uneducated about the effects of what I was doing. I had never heard of chemical dependency. I had never heard the term withdrawal before. I had no idea what addiction was or that people could die from doing what I was doing. All I knew was that I enjoyed getting high.

Before I knew it, I was addicted to pain medication, which eventually kicked off my doctor shopping to get as many of the most powerful drugs that I could get my hands on. Following that was my transformation from pill head to heroin addict. My tolerance for opiates became so high that I could no longer afford pills from the streets, so I switched to heroin. I did not intentionally switch to heroin, however. One day, I simply could not find any pills to buy, so I went into withdrawal and ended up getting some heroin just so that I could feel a little bit better.

As I mentioned, there was a process that I went through to get to where I ended up. It all began as a SOCIAL thing. Just doing it occasionally with friends. Then it progressed into a HABIT where I would do pills every weekend. As my habit continued, it eventually progressed into a full ADDICTION where I could not stop. I was no longer able to wait until the weekend to use. There was no more choice in the matter. I had to use to function. I had to use to get out of bed, to eat, to sleep, and to interact with other people.

SOCIAL> HABIT> ADDICTION

Based on this information, yes, it started out as a choice. Although I was completely uneducated about the effects of long-term opiate use, I still knew that what I was doing was wrong, and I knew that it probably was not good for me. Yet, I continued to use anyway. When my social use moved into a habit, I could see it happening. I knew that my tolerance and frequency was increasing. I still could have stopped myself at this stage. Maybe I would have had some minor withdrawal symptoms such as sleeplessness, a runny nose, or some shakes, but it would have been possible to stop on my own. Once I progressed into the addiction stage, all choice was gone. It was over for me, and opiates now called the shots. Unfortunately, I do not know how long I spent in each of the three stages. That is the tricky part, for I have no idea when I became addicted. Having said that, I would strongly suggest seeking treatment no matter what stage you or your loved one is in. There is no need to wait until they have a criminal record to get them help. There is no sense in waiting until they have stolen everything from you to get them help. If they are in the social stage, then get them help before they reach the habit stage. If they are in the habit stage, then get them help before they reach the addiction stage. If they are in the addiction stage, then for the love of God, get them help before they die.

When it comes to other drugs, my experience is much different. Take marijuana, for example. I smoked pot for years and never got addicted to it. Based on my own experience, I will strongly argue that marijuana is not addictive. However, I do believe that it is habit-forming. Take my addiction model, for example. Social> Habit> Addiction. My marijuana use began as a social thing. My high school friends were all doing it, and I wanted to fit in. Then it moved up to a habit. Rather than only using on weekends with friends like it used to be, I was now smoking every day. It was a habit to smoke before and after school. It was a habit to smoke while we were in Kyle's garage playing pool. It was a habit to smoke before we went out to see a movie. The difference is that I never stole for pot. I was never homeless or sent to rehab for it. I certainly never attempted suicide because of it. Although I was using it every day, it did not have a grasp on me or my decision making like opiates did. When I decided to quit smoking pot, I did. I made the decision that I simply did not want to use it anymore. Marijuana was getting stronger and stronger, and it caused me to be lazy. The only downside to it was that it took me a week or so to get used to sleeping without it. Just like popping your knuckles or chewing your fingernails, it took time and a little bit of effort to quit, but I did it on my own, without treatment, and it never progressed into an addiction.

The same could be said about cocaine. Cocaine was my first love when it came to drugs. I used the drug for years because of the incredible high that it produced. Again, it started off as a social thing. My friend Pete introduced me to it, and at first, I would only use it with him. However, it, too, became a habit when I began to use it on my own. Cocaine was definitely not as harsh on my life as opiates were, but it took far more of a toll on me than marijuana. If you read or have heard me tell my story before, then you know that cocaine broke me financially. Not only did it hurt my bank account, but it also impacted my friendships and schooling. Then again, I will credit those struggles to poor decision making, not the drug itself. The only time that coke affected my decision making was when I was high on it. If it was in my system, I craved more of it, and especially after I ran out and I was coming down off the high. But, the next morning was always a fresh start. Opiates, on the other hand, I was always addicted to. I was always craving it. My coke use stopped when I made the decision to never touch it again. Just like marijuana, I quit on my own with no withdrawal or rehab.

Now for alcohol. There is a saying that I once heard from an old friend of mine from Alcoholics Anonymous. "An alcoholic is born. An addict is made". Personally, I never really struggled with alcohol. I drank a lot through my teens and early twenties, but I never became dependent on it. My alcohol seemed to have gotten stuck in the social stage. I say social stage rather than habit because, even though I drank every single day as a freshman in college, once I moved out of that apartment and into my own apartment, my drinking slowed down tremendously. Once I was living by myself, I only drank when I had friends over to play cards or to grill out. Other than that, the alcohol that I had would just sit in the refrigerator.

Being a member of Alcoholics Anonymous for as long as I was, I met a lot of people and heard a lot of stories. After hearing the stories, I would most certainly agree that the statement "alcoholics are born" is true. All "real" alcoholics that I know personally have very similar stories. They took their first sip of alcohol at a very young age and have craved it ever since. As they grew older, once the alcohol hit their lips, something would have to stop them from drinking. They would be completely unable to stop on their own. They would either have to drink until the bar closed, drink until they passed out or until they were arrested. They would drink at work, before work, after work, while they ate, as soon as they opened their eyes in the morning and would continue all day. Then, they would do it all over again the next day. They would drink to sleep, to wake up, and to stop themselves from shaking. You can make an addict out of anyone. Give them opiates for a few weeks and they will eventually become dependent on it. Alcohol, on the other hand, seems to vary from person to person.

There is a second statement that I was taught while I was in treatment, which was "if you are an addict, you are an alcoholic. If you are an alcoholic, you are an addict". This theory I disagreed with but did not question until I was around 3 years sober. As I wrote this book, I asked myself many questions that I wanted to answer. One of the questions was, is that true? Determined to know the answer, I decided to test that theory on myself. While Megan and I were eating out at an Italian restaurant, I told her what my question was and was open with her about the fact that I did not know if I drank alcohol if I would be able to stop. I also told her that I did not really know if I would eventually turn back to opiates if I drank. I did, however, tell her signs to watch out for and the reasoning behind why I did not believe that anything bad was going to happen. After our conversation, I reached over and took a sip of her wine. Nothing happened. After leaving the restaurant, we stopped by a liquor store and bought a 6-pack of beer, which we drank together that night. Still, nothing happened. I have drunk alcohol ever since, proving that, no, being addicted to opiates does not automatically make you an alcoholic.

Let me be very clear. I would never recommend an addict or someone in recovery to attempt to drink alcohol. I did it because I wanted to provide information to the reader of this book. Over the past few years, I have drunk socially. There have been a few occasions where I would drink too much or drink 3 or 4 nights in a row. But then again, I cannot think of anyone who drinks alcohol who has not had one too many every now and again. Regardless, I have never returned to using other drugs, nor have I found myself *needing* to drink for any reason. I drink because, well, I can do so successfully like a normal human being.

My final thought about whether it is a choice or not is yes and no. Of course, it is a choice to take the first hit or the first drink. It is a choice to hang out with a group of people who you know you probably should not be around. But, eventually, the choice no longer exists. Diabetes can start with a choice to eat unhealthily and not exercise. Lung cancer can start with a choice to smoke cigarettes. Mouth cancer can start with a choice to dip or chew tobacco. Oh, and do not forget that many addicts started off just like me. They were given a prescription from their trusted doctor with no information or knowledge about what they were taking. Most of the heroin addicts that we have were made by legal opiate pain killers.

The social stage is a choice. The habit stage may or may not be a choice. The addiction stage most certainly is not! Either way, it does not matter. Addiction is a problem regardless of your feelings on the subject, and addicts need help!

Does it Ever Go Away?

No. The thought to use may never go away, but it does get easier to control. Much easier.

Based on my own experience and after speaking to thousands of other addicts, the desire to find that once enjoyable high never seems to leave the addict. It simply becomes more manageable over time. While the drug is being abused, the addict's tolerance continues to grow, which then forces the addict to use more of the drug to achieve the same feeling. For heroin addicts, the high eventually becomes impossible to achieve and is then only being used to function or "feel normal." This is due to the drug causing the brain to release a massive amount of dopamine, a neurotransmitter that plays a major role in the reward center of the brain. Over time of abstinence, the levels in the brain can return to almost normal. However, the memory of the high will remain. And because the memory of the euphoric feeling remains, there will always be the risk of relapse.

Now, let us take the drug away from the addict. After detoxification, what is left? People who sold them the drugs and people that they used to use with. Places where they used to get high or purchase drugs. Places that they used to steal from. Things, like what they would pawn for drug money. Maybe something as common as a spoon. Also, memories. The memory of the good times that they had. Memories of the high. Memories of what they had done to themselves or to others in order to get high. Everywhere, there will be reminders of their past as a drug addict.

People

    This was a tough one for me because I had many childhood friends who were still using drugs after I had gotten clean. The friendships that I made in the circle in the woods, many of them were still drinking and smoking pot. This was fine for them. They were able to do it and still live their lives successfully. But, at the beginning of my recovery, I simply could not be around any of them. There were many weddings, get-togethers, outings, and cook-outs that I had to pass up because I did not feel comfortable or confident enough. It was hard for me to cut them out of my life, but it was also very necessary in order for me to maintain my sobriety. My point is that it is imperative to stay clear from people who you know are still using. Cut ties with them completely. Do not keep their phone numbers, and do not remain friends with them on social media. It will be a difficult thing to do, for it can easily be justified. But, it is not worth the risk, especially at the beginning of sobriety.

    There were other people who I needed to cut out of my life entirely, like the dope boys. I deleted all of their phone numbers out of my phone. They would still have my phone number, though, and they would still reach out to me from time to time. My goal was to put as many walls up between them and me as I could. I made sure to clean out my friends list on social media, as well. As time went on, they would eventually stop contacting me. The cool thing about all of this was that people used to contact me because they wanted to get high. Now, if I hear from them, it is because they are wanting to get sober. Something that I must warn you of, however, is that if you are newly sober and someone reaches out to you for help, I would strongly suggest that you take someone with you when you go to help that person. Far too many times have I heard of a newly sober heroin addict go help a friend of theirs who is still using and then relapsing themselves. Their intentions may be pure, but they were still too new in their recovery to try and help someone else on their own. So be careful. Now that I am more confident in myself, I am now able to associate with my old friends who still smoke pot or drink. I can go to weddings and parties without the fear of snorting something or sticking a needle into my vein.

Places

This one is a little trickier than people. With people, you can control who you talk to or hang out with. You can remove phone numbers or friends from your friends list. You can filter who calls you. You can choose to text back or not. But, you cannot literally remove places. You can, however, control where you go. As I mentioned, weddings were a big one for me. Early in my recovery, I did not feel comfortable going to weddings. There are generally two reasons why people go to weddings, which are to dance and to drink an unlimited amount of alcohol. I did not do either of them early in my recovery, so I did my best to avoid going to a wedding wherever I could. In the event where I did have to go, then I would attach myself to someone that I trusted. Someone who knew my struggles and my story, like my girlfriend, Megan. It was important for me to be with someone who would hold me accountable and who would be there for me when I needed them to be.

There were other places within the city that I would avoid, as well. All of my dope came from Cincinnati, so I was, and still am, very careful about which part of Cincinnati I go to. As time has gone one, I have become more and more comfortable with being in certain places. Toward the beginning of my recovery, just the sight of Downtown Cincinnati made my stomach turn. Now, I can find the beauty in the city and actually enjoy it. Time can be a powerful tool.

Things

Just like with places, the things that could be considered a "trigger" for a recovering addict were everywhere. For me, it was the car that I used to live in, needles when I get my blood drawn at the doctor's office, and my mother's jewelry box. These things I just had to deal with, to be honest with you. All I can say is that they are just objects. Unfortunately, these objects served a different purpose for me than what they were originally intended. Such as the laptop or my Xbox. When I got sober, I learned to enjoy them the way that they were supposed to be enjoyed. I continuously had to tell myself that they were not the problem. They had no control over me. Then I slowly started to have healthy relationships with them.

Memories

To me, memories are, by far, the hardest part about recovery. The memory or the high. The memory of "the good ol' days" when it was still fun. The memory of all of the terrible things that I did to my friends and family. The memory of all of the friends who have died because of an overdose. The memory of Kyle. The memory of the look in his father's eyes.

A lot of the memories lost their power over me once I finally addressed them. Such as the lying and stealing that I did to my parents. Those things really ate me up inside, but the guilt that I had carried around with me for so long disappeared once I admitted my faults and sincerely apologized for them. Making amends to those that have been hurt is a great way to deal with guilt and shame for what I had done to them. I do not think that it is a coincidence that this is a huge step in 12-step programs. While I was going through the steps of Alcoholics Anonymous, I was able to use the fourth step to write down all of the things that bothered me about my past. The fifth step allowed me to get out all of my secrets and tell them to another person who I trusted. The eighth step was making a list of all of the people and places that I had harmed, and the ninth step gave me the opportunity to make amends to them. This is how I dealt with my memories.

Other memories are a bit harder to deal with, however. Like the memory of the first time that I shot heroin. It sounds crazy, but even though heroin destroyed my life and nearly killed me, part of me still cannot help but think about that first time. The good time, before I was homeless or suicidal. I know what will happen to me if I ever use again, so I won't. But, over the years of speaking to other heroin addicts, it is not uncommon for them to tell me that they relapsed because they felt like they could control it next time. It never works out that way. After the withdrawal is over, the addict's mind then becomes his or her worst enemy. This is where rigorous honesty comes into play. The addict must know that the high that they experienced the first time will never be matched again. They must know that there is no such thing as a social heroin addict. If you are addicted to drugs, or if you are an alcoholic, you may never be able to use successfully. The odds are not in your favor, so please, do not try. Justifying this can kill you!

The memory of Kyle is the hardest for me to deal with. Right now, as I write this, it has been nearly three years since I found him in that Walmart parking lot, and I still have not been able to forgive myself. Yes, he made his own decision to relapse. It was his choice to take those pills from that guy he worked with. It was his choice to seek out heroin after that. What I struggle with, however, is that he begged me for help and I did nothing. I witnessed him crying in front of me, and I did nothing. He did what he was supposed to do and reached out to me, the person that he trusted with his very life, and I let him down. There was no goodbye, only the thought of "what if?". I think about him every single day. Although I have not forgiven myself, I deal with this memory by turning the entire situation into a positive. Kyle is now my biggest source of motivation. He is my "WHY," my purpose. All of the time that I spend with other addicts, all of the energy that I put into this, the decision to continue my education, and even this book, are all a product of Kyle; the experiences that I had with him, the regret and the pain that I feel from his passing, are the reasons why I do what I do.

Every addict's people, places, things, and memories will be different. My point to this chapter is to inform you that, even though the drugs are gone, the addict is still challenged every single day with reminders and temptations. No addict will ever be able to fully recover unless they can confront all these issues. There must be a lot of support, patience, understanding, and effort from all involved. The addict will not be able to do this all on their own. They need your support! And, none of this will be easy, but it is most certainly worth it!

What to Look For

As the loved one of an active drug user, there are plenty of signs that you can look for if you have any suspicion. Many times, your gut will be enough. But, if you cannot trust your gut, or do not want to, then keep your eyes peeled. More than likely, these signs will be fairly consistent.

Opiates

Some of the physical signs of opiate abuse will include nausea, vomiting, slow or slurred speech, sluggish movement, drowsiness, and "nodding out," which is when the addict will drift in and out of sleep. It is common for nodding out to occur mid-conversation. You may also notice "track marks" on their arms, hands, or neck. Many times, I would tell people that my dog scratched me, or I would wear long sleeves to keep my arms covered. If your loved one is displaying any of these signs and consistently wearing long sleeves in the middle of summer, then there is a chance that they could be using abusing opiates.

Heroin and other opiates aren't typically called "heroin" or "opiates" on the streets. Some of the common terms used could include boy, tar, black, H, a shot, or dope.

Other things to look for could be powdery residue on flat surfaces such as a sink, desktop, countertop, dresser, nightstand, back of a toilet, a CD case, or a small mirror. Also, keep your eye out for missing spoons, tiny balls of cotton, cellophane from cigarette packs, financial difficulty, or missing items of value such as gaming consoles, televisions, or DVDs. Heroin can be different colors and can look like powder, a rock, like tar, or a piece of drywall. I have seen black, white, gray, brown, tan, and even orange. If you have any suspicion, please be careful. There have been reports of police officers overdosing on heroin, or the more powerful fentanyl, just by coming into contact with it.

Crystal Methamphetamine

This is a powerful stimulant that will cause the user to show many signs of use. Some of the signs may include an abnormal increase in physical activity or energy, dilated pupils, sweating, loss of appetite, paranoia, sleeplessness, uncontrollable picking of the skin, or uncontrollable clenching of the jaw. Potential health risks can include depression, fatigue, anxiety, seizures, violent behavior, or severe weight loss. Over the last decade or so, the drug of choice seems to have been heroin. However, methamphetamine is making one hell of a comeback, so be aware.

Some common names for methamphetamine include ice, meth, crystal, tweek, crank, or speed. More often than not, the substance will look like crystals or like ice. Methamphetamine can be consumed in different forms, as well. It can be smoked, snorted, or injected. Again, be on the lookout for track marks.

Alcohol

Booze can be a little trickier than other drugs. It can no doubt be addictive, but not everyone who drinks will become an alcoholic. Some may abuse alcohol. Some may be hard drinkers. Some may be social drinkers. Some may be real alcoholics. Many people that I have spoken with believe that an alcoholic has been born with a predisposition to alcohol abuse. Basically, the alcoholic may have been an alcoholic before they ever even took a drink. Often, real alcoholics will need to drink when they wake up in the morning to prevent themselves from vomiting or shaking. Many will need to hide their alcohol use from friends and family. Some will hide alcohol around the house and possibly drink while they are at work in order to function. Most of the time, once they begin drinking, they will need to continue to drink until all the alcohol is gone, the bar closes, they pass out, or they are arrested. It is not uncommon that some outside force will need to be the reason for a real alcoholic to stop drinking once they have started.

Someone who abuses alcohol, on the other hand, may just be a heavy drinker. They may drink daily, but still be able to stop before bed, then get up the next morning for work and have no issues at all doing it. Or, they could only drink one night a week, but constantly putting themselves into risky situations, often resulting in different consequences. This person, to me, sounds like a hard drinker.

The tricky part of this is that it is not always clear which category each drinker falls into. Ideally, the drinker himself needs to be the one to make that decision. Either way, some of the signs of a real alcoholic can include loss in interest in work or hobbies, depression, isolation from friends and family, violent or being unable to control how much alcohol is consumed. Also, keep an eye out for slurred speech, vomiting, impaired motor skills, and lack in judgment. As I said, just because they may show some of these signs, this does not necessarily mean that they are an alcoholic. They may just be a hard drinker. So, be careful when confronting your loved one. They may not want to hear the news.

Cocaine

Cocaine and crack cocaine are very similar when it comes to the effect of the drug. Crack cocaine is a freebase form of cocaine and is very cheap, powerful, and fast-acting. The biggest difference in the two is that the high from crack does not last nearly as long as the high from cocaine. Only minutes. Crack cocaine is smoked out of a pipe while cocaine can be smoked, snorted, or injected. Some of the signs of the two are dilated pupils, inability to sleep, muscle twitching, lack of appetite, weight loss, and being over-energetic. Also, the user may be aggressive, have financial difficulty, may be paranoid, and have mood swings.

Cocaine may also be referred to as white, girl, white girl, soft, snow, or powder. Crack is sometimes called hard, rock, yay, or ball.

Marijuana

Pot is another drug that I would like to touch on. It is very common and is even becoming legal for medicinal or recreational use in most areas. Marijuana is most commonly used by smoking or vaping, but can also be eaten. A list of other names that it may be called can include weed, grass, green, ganja, pot, or smoke. Signs of use can include red eyes, heavy eyes, slow movement, increased appetite, and oftentimes has a strong odor.

Marijuana does not seem to have an addicting effect on the user. If you refer back to my Social> Habit< Addicted theory, marijuana never appears to surpass the habit stage. Many users smoke socially. They may smoke daily, but do it with other friends most of the time. Others smoke by themselves in the comfort of their own home. There have been many reasons given for the use of marijuana, such as to relax (being the most common), to sleep, or to make watching a movie or doing other recreational activities more enjoyable. Marijuana is even being prescribed by medical professionals to decrease physical pain, depression, anxiety, or to help the person sleep or increase their appetite.

Loving Versus Enabling

This topic is definitely one of the more difficult when it comes to addiction. Most of the friends and family members that I speak with are completely exhausted due to having to deal with an addicted loved one. They still love the addict. They want to help them, but what does helping look like? When does helping become enabling? This chapter is about exactly that. I will go over some things that I did as a heroin addict, so you have an idea of what to look for. I will also tell you exactly how I was being enabled by my family and how you can avoid doing what they did to me for so many years.

Here are just a few ways that you may be enabling your loved on:

- Giving money

- Bailing them out of jail

- Paying their bills

- Trusting them when they tell you that they will quit, or that "this will be the last time"

- Allowing them to live with you

- Making excuses for them

These are not all the ways that an addict can be enabled; these are just some of the common ways that my parents enabled me. If you are anything like my family, they just wanted to help me, but they did not know how. They also feared what I would do if they cut me off like they wanted to. They would justify giving me money by telling themselves something like, "Well, it's better that he gets it from me instead of going out and stealing for it and getting caught."

In all honesty, though, would jail really be that bad for them? At least then, you would know exactly where they are, they would have food and shelter, and they would have less of a chance of getting drugs. The same goes for them allowing me to live with them. They just could not bear the thought of me living in a box underneath a bridge. I ended up homeless anyway, but it was not because they forced me out.

In my opinion, and this may be one of the most difficult things that you will ever do in your life, the best thing that you can do for your addicted loved one is to completely cut them off. Give them the choice to either get help or get out. More often than not, they will choose to leave instead of getting help. This may seem cruel to you, but the chance of them seeking treatment will remain extremely slim if they know that you will always be there to catch them when they fall. If they know that you will be there to pay their bills, feed them, give them a place to live, and fuel their addiction, why would they ever need to change?

You may have heard the term "rock bottom" before. Although it is not 100% necessary to begin treatment, it does help. If you kick them out of your house, stop giving them money and stop letting them use you, you will be forcing them to fend for themselves, making it more difficult for them to feed their addiction and bringing them closer to "rock bottom" at the same time. When my family finally cut me off, I began to take steps toward recovery without even knowing it. I was beaten down and alone. When I was forced to steal in order to get high, I was caught, arrested, and sent to jail. Jail itself is not where I got my treatment. Getting arrested is very rarely enough to get an addict sober. It was beneficial for me, however, because it forced me to detox. Being in jail also kept me away from it long enough for my head to clear. At that point, I was able to make some rational decisions. My treatment came after jail, from a long-term inpatient rehab and a 12-step program.

As I said, cutting your loved one out of your life will be extremely difficult, but they will not stop if they know that they have you to manipulate. Addicts are masters at lying and manipulating, so be cautious. Especially if they are in withdrawal. But, please be ready to help them when that time comes. You will know when that time comes when they come to you and say something like, "I need help," or "I can't do this anymore." Remember, that window of opportunity that you have to help the addict is very, very small. If they come to you and show even the slightest sign of interest in getting help, stop what you are doing and help them. Be prepared. Gather information so that you know how to get them into treatment.

Do not forget my experience with Kyle. When he reached out to me for help, I put him on hold. I was not prepared, and I did not think that I would never see him again. Kyle overdosed and died within just a couple of days as a result of me not being ready to help him. Then, my window of opportunity slammed shut. Do not make the same mistake that I made.

Relapse

Some recovery models say that relapse is a part of recovery. I do not completely agree, although relapse can be a great learning opportunity.

Being in recovery for as long as I have, I have heard many stories as to why people relapse. Some report relapsing because their lives were terrible. They lost their job, their home, their relationship, so they relapsed to numb the pain that they were feeling at the time. Any other stressful situation you can think of can, and probably has been used as an excuse to relapse. On the other hand, I have also heard many recovering addicts say that they relapsed because their life was too good. They got a car, landed a good job, saved up a good amount of money, mended broken relationships, and anything else that normal people do daily. They saw this as a reason to celebrate their accomplishments, so they used. Or, they begin to think that they have cured their addiction, and, for some reason, it is now safe to use. This may not make a lot of sense to you, but when you live the life of an addict, the world becomes a very dark and negative place. When an addict gets sober, they begin to be happy, accountable, and productive. They then feel like they have earned it and decide to treat themselves with a drink or a couple of pills. Others start to think that they are now normal because of their success, so they try to use again. "I thought enough time had gone by that I would be alright this time." I hear this quite often.

From my own experience with relapse, I look back and realize that I was simply unprepared for the major events that life was throwing at me. Before my relapse, I was in jail for a month before being sent straight to inpatient treatment for another ten months. Nearly the entire year that I was sober, I was sheltered from the "real world." Once I left treatment, I was forced to face the passing of my grandfather and my son's heart surgery. I did not know how to handle these situations. In the past, I had always run away from problems like these and numbed the pain by using drugs. Now that I was sober, what do I do? Being fresh out of rehab, vulnerable and unprepared, I relapsed. Even sober, I ended up doing what I had always done. The good thing about my relapse, however, was that I was able to learn from it.

Relapse is possibly the most powerful way for an addict to learn. If they are able to survive a relapse and obtain sobriety once more, it is very possible for them to use their relapse as a tool to prevent them from another relapse in the future. Relapse does not mean failure! Today, I know that there are other ways to deal with stressful situations in life. I also know that situations like the ones that I went through will continue to happen throughout the rest of my life. I did things daily in order to get high. Now I have to do things daily in order to remain clean.

I am one of the lucky ones, though. Not everyone who relapses lives to learn from it. I have had many friends and clients of mine overdose because of their relapse. Some survived, others did not. Many times, what will happen is that they will get clean for several months, or years even, before they decide to use again. Because of the length of time that they had been sober, their tolerance for the drug was much lower than it used to be, and they will not know how much to use. Then, they will use too much and overdose. Another thing that I have noticed is that when they get sober, they will lose contact with the drug dealer that they are familiar with. When they relapse, they will end up going to a different dope boy with no idea how strong the drug is. Also, if you have been keeping up with the news, heroin is fading away. Unfortunately, it is being replaced with fentanyl and carfentanyl. These two drugs are extremely powerful synthetic opiates and are responsible for killing a lot of the addicts that I know personally.

My point to all of this is to inform you of two things. One, relapse is very dangerous. Two, it can be a powerful learning tool for you and your loved one. If your loved one relapses, remain patient and willing to help them. You may feel hopeless, let down, angry, confused, hurt, shocked, or scared, but do not give up. If your loved one is alive, there is hope that they will get clean again. Seek out a support network. Know that relapse can happen repeatedly and can range from a one time "slip," to years of continuous use. Find support. Prepare yourself. Have a plan in place, and remain willing and hopeful.

Treatment Options

There are a number of programs and treatment options available for addicts to receive help. These can range from total abstinence, 12-step programs such as Alcoholics Anonymous and Narcotics Anonymous, inpatient facilities, outpatient services, and Medication-Assisted Treatment. There are no programs that work 100% for everyone. Some can get sober by just attending 12-step meetings. Others, like myself, need to go to a long-term inpatient facility. But, there are benefits to be had from all of them.

Twelve-step programs

These types of programs can be very beneficial when it comes to getting sober. The most common are Alcoholics Anonymous and Narcotics Anonymous. Twelve-step meetings are generally abstinence-based programs that are based around the belief in a higher power. Each of the 12 steps is spiritual in nature, and if done with sincerity, can change an addict's thinking and actions. Alcoholics Anonymous has been around since 1935 and has helped millions of people put an end to their drinking problem. Narcotics Anonymous was first introduced in 1953 and is modeled off the twelvesteps of Alcoholics Anonymous. It, too, has helped a countless amount of people.

My experience with 12-step programs has had a profound impact on my recovery and my life. I have worked through the steps multiple times, and each time I was able to take a closer look at myself, which led to more changes. One of the great things about 12-step programs is that the program forces the member to focus on themselves rather than pointing their finger at other people. As addicts, many of us have lived our lives pretending to be a victim of the cruel world that we live in. The steps stripped me of that luxury and forced me to find my part in the situations where I felt like a victim. By keeping the focus on myself and finding my part, I was then able to figure out what I could have done differently. How could I have handled that situation better? Why did this particular statement hurt my feelings? Why did I feel like everyone was out to get me? The steps allowed me to see that my thoughts and actions were the reason why I ended up the way that I did, and once I was able to accept responsibility rather than placing the blame on the rest of the world, then I was able to change. This is not an easy thing to do, however. It takes a lot of courage and willingness to admit to yourself and someone else just how messed up you are. It is easy to point your finger at everyone else and point out everyone else's faults, but you can only change once you admit to yourself that maybe you need to change.

Another great thing about 12-step programs is the relationships that can be formed. These programs are completely reliant on the members to keep them operating. There is not a boss or a corporate representative instructing the groups on how to operate. The members lean on each other. They rely on one another for support and guidance. And the best part, they are all there for the same reason you are! Knowing this really took a lot of the pressure off me when I was asking for help. Everything that I had been through, I was able to seek out someone else who had done the exact same things that I had. This made me feel comfortable enough to open up and get honest with other people for once. Let me tell you, being that vulnerable with another person can create bonds and friendships that will never be broken.

There are countless numbers of 12-step meetings all over the world. No matter what area that you live in, there is more than likely a meeting that is within driving distance from you. For a list of Alcoholics Anonymous meetings in your area, visit www.aa.org. For a list of Narcotics Anonymous meetings, visit www.na.org. The websites also offer literature and many other resources for you to use. They are there to help!

Inpatient Treatment

Inpatient treatment programs, also known as residential treatment, are quickly popping up all over the country to battle addiction. Taking advantage of inpatient treatment allows the addict to remove themselves from "the real world," giving them time to focus on themselves. These programs typically provide access to counselors and case managers who are there to help the addict cope with recovery and to help prepare them for their transition back into life by giving them resources for jobs, housing, transportation, insurance, and many other things. Normally, there is a strict schedule to be followed daily but will also allow more freedoms and privileges as they progress through the program. Inpatient treatment can last anywhere from 10 days to one year.

Residential treatment is a huge reason that I am still alive today. For most of my life, I had no structure or routine. I did what I wanted, when I wanted. I had no responsibly. Inpatient taught me structure. It taught me to go to bed at a reasonable hour and to wake up at a normal time. It taught me how to do chores, make my bed, and how to be responsible. This was a big deal for me. These things may seem like normal things to do, but I was a heroin addict, and most heroin addicts that I know are not too worried about making their bed or cleaning their bathroom sink. Inpatient was also the reason why I met some of the most influential people in my life today. One of the greatest gifts that a recovering addict must give is their support and experience. The people in recovery that were serious about remaining sober made it a point to visit the clients in residential treatment to offer them their support. Not only that, but the other clients that I was in the program with played a major role in my recovery. We were all there for the same reason, so we were able to rely on each other for support and for advice whenever it was needed. I was locked up in a house with 120 other addicts for nine months, which forced me to bond with them and make new friendships with sober people. Until then, I had zero friends who were sober, and it was needed.

Outpatient Treatment

Outpatient treatment is much less intensive than inpatient treatment. Unlike inpatient, outpatient allows the addict to remain at their home, continue to work, go to school, and handle any other responsibilities that they may have. Treatment will generally include group counseling, individual counseling, and will focus more on education about addiction. A normal session can last for three hours and may be required for up to five days per week. Completion of outpatient can be obtained after the required course material has been learned in combination with a certain amount of group and individual sessions attended. On average, outpatient treatment can be completed in three to six months but can last up to a year or longer, depending on the level of care needed by the patient.

Although inpatient is not a requirement to attend outpatient, it is common for one to transition to outpatient once they complete inpatient. After I moved back home from treatment, I decided to attend a weekly outpatient program that my rehab facility offered. Once a week, I would go back to the facility for a group counseling session. This helped me remain accountable in my recovery and gave me the opportunity to reach out for help to the guys that I went through inpatient with. Personally, I needed to be in inpatient, but my heroin use was extremely severe. Outpatient would be a good fit for someone with a mild to moderate substance use disorder.

Medication-Assisted Treatment

Medication-Assisted Treatment (MAT) is the use of medications that have been approved by the FDA. These medications are then often used in combination with group and individual counseling sessions. I want to stress the importance of the word "assisted" in MAT. The medication is only an aid in the recovery process. Does this mean that you aren't really sober if you take a MAT medication? It does not matter! The medication allows time for relationships to be rebuilt. For homes to be repaired. It allows time for the addicted person to obtain employment, get their GED, get into college, pay off their fines and restitution, to catch up on their child support. The medication does not cure the disease. The medication simply gives the opportunity to take control of life.

The most common medications used are Methadone, Naltrexone, and Buprenorphine. Buprenorphine, or more commonly known as Suboxone, comes in the form of a tablet or a film that dissolves under the tongue or in the cheek. This medication has been making a huge impact when used properly in treating addiction. Suboxone is used to help alleviate the withdrawal symptoms of opiates and contains an "opiate blocker." This means that while the Suboxone is in the system, if the addict attempts to use an opiate, the Suboxone will block the euphoric effect and reverse it, putting the addict into withdrawal. Over time, the addict and doctor will wean the patient off the medication. Methadone, on the other hand, does not block the effects of opiates. If it is used properly, it can greatly help an addict with their withdrawal symptoms, but unlike Suboxone, Methadone will build up in the system and the dosage will have to be increased.

If you read my story, you will know that my experience with Medication-Assisted Treatment is limited. I attempted to use Suboxone once, but I misused it and lied to my doctor, which led me straight into an even worse withdrawal than I was already in. However, I currently work very closely with doctors' offices who provide MAT, primarily Suboxone and Vivitrol. I have seen the medication work for thousands of patients. Personally, I believe that total abstinence is the way to go. But, with the overdose rate rising, the death rate increasing, and heroin transitioning to fentanyl, I believe that if MAT is available to keep people alive, then I am all for it. Remember what I said, as long as they are still breathing, then there is hope.

Family & Friend Support

If you are a family member or a friend of an addicted loved one, you will no doubt need some support as well. Luckily, there are plenty of options for you. My parents were affected by my addiction just as much as I was. They lost sleep. They were depressed and stressed out to the max. They lived every day waiting for the news that their only son was dead. They lived in a constant state of fear. My parents turned to their church and to Al-Anon.

Al-Anon is a support group that was designed to help loved ones understand their loved one's alcoholism and provided them with education and resources so that they can recover themselves. Addiction is commonly referred to as a "family disease," meaning that it is not only the addict who is affected, but also their family. Much like Alcoholics Anonymous, Al-anon is operated by other people who are going through the same thing that you are. It is simply a group of people who are willing to be open and honest with each other. They are there to support one another and offer each other strength and hope. It is important for you to know that there is little that you can do to keep your loved one from using drugs or alcohol. Al-anon is there to help you learn how to live and be happy, whether your loved one is sober or not.

Alateen is another support group that is designed to bring understanding and coping skills to the children of an addict or alcoholic. The parents or partners are not the only ones who suffer. The children do, as well. Alateen is much like Al-Anon in that it is a group of normal teenagers who come together to support one another and to offer strength and hope. You can gather more information and find meeting schedules for both programs by visiting www.al-anon.org.

There are numerous support groups available for you and your loved one. The options that I have listed are not the only ones that are available to you, they are simply the most common and the largest. Some people turn to church, to other family members, psychiatrists, doctors, or any other professional that they may trust. It is important to find who or what works best for you and is relevant to what you are going through. This is not something to mess around with, so please take it seriously.

They are Sober... Now What?

Once your loved one is sober, you may think that the battle is finally over. "I'm so glad they are finally past that part of their life," you might say. I am sorry to have to tell you, but that is simply not true. The battle is far from over. Early sobriety is tough! The choice in friends must change. They will be vulnerable in certain places or situations. For example, I had a difficult time at weddings because I seemed to be the only one in attendance that was not completely intoxicated. I also struggled with being in Downtown Cincinnati. It took me years to replace all of my horrific memories from Cincinnati with new, fun, and even beautiful memories. Furthermore, it will take a lot of time, patience, effort, and understanding from all people involved to get through the first few months of sobriety. Your loved one may seem distant. They may seem like they feel out of place. They may need to go to a 12-step meeting abruptly, which may cause you to question, "Are they really going to a meeting, or are they going to get drugs?" Early sobriety will be a transitional period for everyone.

What helped me get back on track was a combination of many things. 12-step meetings and my sponsor helped me a lot, especially in the beginning. Getting into college and finding a direction for my life was huge. Going to the gym and exercising on a regular basis played a significant role as it helped me fill my free time and built my confidence. Too much free time can be dangerous for a newly sober person, so it is very important for them to find a hobby and really focus on self-care. Eventually, getting back into the church has opened my eyes to many instances where God kept me alive over the years. Continuing to grow in my faith has become an essential part of my recovery. These are just a few contributing factors to my success in recovery. I really want to stress the importance of finding something to focus on. That could be finding a job, sponsoring people, volunteering at your local homeless shelter, church, the gym, enrolling in college or obtaining you GED, rock climbing, wood-working, writing, coloring, or buying a puppy. Anything that is productive and enjoyable.

Perhaps the biggest help for me was the support from the people who love me the most. My mother, father, and my wife. It was important for them to remain patient and understanding of the changes and adjustments that I needed to make. This next section was written by my parents, Paul and Cheryl, and my wife, Megan.

My Wife's Experience

I met Matt when he was only four months sober. Before then, I had never had any type of relationship with someone in recovery. He was actually a resident at Campbell County Jail when we met. As a naïve 23-year-old, I had no idea what work release meant. Even after I found out, there was still something so special about him. He had a soft, sad twinkle in his eye that was looking to be found.

Before our first date, I told my mom I was going because Matt just needed a positive person in his life. A three-hour walk and talk, followed by ice cream, and I was hooked. The simple and open heart of someone newly sober is so unique. Although an issue that quickly became apparent is that I was becoming his new drug. At first, it was awesome to always feel wanted and needed, but we moved fast. After just two weeks, he told me he loved me. Within five months, we moved in together. Looking back, I should have done a better job of setting boundaries. Matt was so thirsty to feel loved, supported, and needed. He needed a purpose, and for a while, I became that purpose. It created an unhealthy balance in our relationship and isolated us from our friends. Matt, who had burned most of his bridges while active in addition, didn't have many, if any, friends at all. So my friendships suffered. You and your loved one won't grow in isolation. A.A. was really his only source of outside support and community. It really helped him reflect on his character flaws and motivated him to live a better life. Addicts face a huge battle with selfishness. Just imagine going to the level of stealing from your loved ones to get high. The longer that behavior is cultivated, the harder it is to reverse. When Matt stopped going to A.A., it put a halt on his personal growth. He then had to work on self-reflection, which, as we all know, isn't the easiest and requires lots of practice. Most all of us struggle with selfish tendencies. Matt has improved drastically in the last six years. There are still times when I'm taken aback by his selfish perspective, and I openly communicate my concerns. That is my biggest piece of advice for anyone building, creating, mending a relationship with someone in recovery. **OPEN COMMUNICATION.** Learn how to love and support through constructive criticism. Show grace and have faith that each year will get easier.

Anyone who has been in active addiction misses out on a lot of crucial maturation. Matt used drugs from ages 13-16. A lot of learning and growing happened during those years. When I realized what all he had missed out on, it helped me better understand his social anxiety. Matt still struggles with certain social cues and interactions, and we just laugh about it now.

For the first three or four years, there was a lot of worry that he would use again, and it ate me up. Eventually, I had to learn to let go of the worry and the control and give it to God. Learning to trust Matt was difficult. Even though I did not know him during his active addiction, I knew enough about the Devil that he invited into his heart. Matt is also such a smooth talker, and I'm a very gullible gal. That, in combination with what I knew he was capable of based on his past, kept the possibility of him relapsing always in the back of my mind. I had to equip myself with more God, and the book, "Codependent No More," by Melody Beattie.

When Matt was three years sober, he decided to drink again. As I said, open communication is crucial. He was up-front and honest with me before he drank. At first, I thought, "Yes! Now we won't have to hang out in the coffee section when we go to weddings!" I then began to overthink, "Do I need to start hiding my cash stash?" His choice came with a lot of judgment from friends and family, but Matt was confident that his addiction began and ended with street drugs, not alcohol.

Getting accustomed to alcohol in our relationship was difficult. The drinking escalated for both of us quickly. I personally have had struggles with alcoholism off and on in my life. There were a lot of nights that we would drink beer or go to bars just because we had some free time. Any reason that we could think of to drink, we did. Still, there was only once when Matt got out of control in our first year of drinking. That wasn't the concern, though. It was the habit that was forming. I was most alarmed when he drank five nights in a row. Matt had shared his theory of

Social>Haibt>Addicted with me. His drinking began as a social thing. It helped him feel more comfortable around my old friends, who I had missed over the years. But I saw Matt slipping through the social stage and entering the habit stage. Again, Open Communication! I voiced my concern about his drinking moving into the habit stage. Initially, he did not want to receive my input, but his drinking slowed down. This is still a conversation that we have about once every six to eight months. I know that having a drink or two throughout the week may be common for some, but for an addict in recovery, it could be a slippery slope.

It is not our job to point out all of their mistakes. I do my best to provide Matt with constructive feedback if I think that it is necessary and that it might make him a better person. Our loved ones who are recovering need to feel loved and supported. My first job as Matt's friend, girlfriend, fiancée, and now wife, has always been to encourage him. To remind him that he deserves the best this world has to offer. Addicts don't need a caretaker or an enabler. They need to be kept honest and humble. I am happy to say I do not worry about Matt using heroin at all anymore. He has truly transformed. My advice, if you are dating an addict or are in any kind of relationship with an addict, is this: get into a church and help your loved one find strength in something or someone greater. Encourage them that they are capable of change. Believe in them until they believe in themselves. Miracles happen every day. Help them find their passion. Exercise is great for someone in recovery. Addicts are endorphin junkies, and they need to fill their minds with positive activities like weight lifting, hiking, skateboarding, music, art, et cetera. What did the addict in your life love before drugs or alcohol?

Being with someone who used to be addicted to a substance definitely has its challenges. But, boy, does it have its positives! It is so inspiring to be with someone who has to overcome so many temptations every day. Being with Matt has really helped me fight my own demons. I catch myself thinking, "If Matt can overcome heroin addiction, I can say no to sugar," or, "If he can overcome his addiction, then I can learn how to clean up after myself." Still working on that :-)

Not everyone makes it out of their addiction alive. Not everyone can climb out of "rock bottom." But Matt did. He is a flipping inspiration. Honestly, after six years of being free from his addiction, I tend to forget just how far he has come. But when I do, I am overcome with amazement of how strong he really is.

God does not make mistakes. He is using Matt to inspire and help others get out of their own Hell It's possible. Just believe.

Megan

A Father's View

Grief is defined as deep sorrow, especially that caused by someone's death. As Matt's parents, we felt our son was slowly dying. At first, we had no idea what was going on, but later, we became more educated, and his behavior became more erratic. We watched our only child decline in health. He told us that he was eating enough, but his facial features were changing. He always wore long sleeve shirts or a sweatshirt, so it was hard to look at his frame to determine his weight. But there were other behavioral changes. He was absent from all family activities. He slept late. He did not come home until early in the morning. He would also sneak out of the house through a window in the middle of the night after his mother and I would go to bed. He was always complaining, argumentative, and never happy. As I was writing our memories, it occurred to me that I do not remember Matt being happy or smiling during his teen years. Matt used to be an "A and B" student at school, but his grades also began to decline.

The sneaking out at night and the lack of laughter were the two changes that impacted me the most. Trust and laughter had always been an important part of our home. Because we were a trusting family, it took a long time for his mother and me to catch on to what was happening. Since Matt was an only child, we had nothing with which to compare his behaviors. Our friends were connected to the church and were not sharing similar experiences with their children. We thought his mood swings and behavioral changes were related to growing pains and a boy growing into a man. But trust began to erode the more Matt snuck out of the house. "Why was he doing this?" "What was he doing?" "Where was he going?" Eventually, I nailed the window shut. I raked the mulch outside his window so that I could see fresh footprints. When I got up in the middle of the night, I began to go downstairs to his bedroom to check on him. My phone calls to him would go unanswered, and the next day we would argue about his disappearance. As a hospice chaplain, I had to be on call for emergencies. Often, I would return home in the middle of the night and find Matt missing.

Matt was not the only thing missing. Tools, DVDs, jewelry, gas reserved for the mower, and money...lots of money... were all missing. We would ask for an explanation, but none could be given. I remember on one occasion that Matt came home from work and claimed he put his pay on the dresser, but he could not find it. He blamed his dog for eating it and asked us to help him out. We loved Matt so much, but our trust in him was slipping away.

Another issue that was slipping away was happiness in our home. As a Christian family, joy was an important factor in our home. We argued, we yelled, we stressed, we worried. We were not sleeping. We cried. I cannot tell you how many nights we cried ourselves to sleep. What is ironic is that I was addicted to Ambien in order to sleep while our son was addicted to heroin.

When Matt relapsed, but before his final arrest, we allowed Matt into the house, but by our rules. He could have a change of clothes, a hot shower, and free food. We were comforted that he had at least these three things. When he came home, before he went to his bedroom, he had to strip to his underwear and give us his clothes. We searched his pockets and his room before and after. Once we went to bed, he had to leave. He said he would sleep in his car, but we knew he would eventually leave our driveway and meet up with someone. Soon he stopped coming home altogether. Where was he? Is he safe? Is he in jail? Is he dead? We did not know. The not knowing produced the grief. The grief produced the tears.

There were two very difficult moments for me as a father. It was a Thursday evening, and Matt was home for a change. He confided in us that he was depressed and had thought about suicide. When I asked him if he had a plan, he responded that he would drive his car into an embankment, truck, or tree. He agreed to go to the emergency room.

When we arrived, we were checked into the room without a doorknob on the inside of the room. I believe Matt soon realized he was in over his head. I remember a social worker coming in to talk with him in private and concluded that, yes, Matt had suicidal thoughts. He was admitted to the psych ward for observation.

The next day, I went to visit him and was met by a discharge nurse. She informed me that Matt had succeeded in their tests and was ready to go home. I blew my top. I insisted on speaking to the social worker and nurse manager. I explained that Matt was a master at lying and manipulating and that he would say anything to get his way. I argued how could their social worker on Thursday night assess that Matt is suicidal, and the next day another social worker claim that he is fine? She called the medical director, and the order was changed. Matt had no idea what was happening, but when he found out he was not going to be discharged, he blew his top. I hugged him, told him I loved him, and started toward the door. I still remember his pleading with me to take him home. I knew if I turned around, I would take him home, so I just kept walking. Once I left the facility, the tears flowed uncontrollably.

The second difficult moment came after he left the detox center, broke into the house, and stole the car and the laptop. We had already filed Casey's Law on his behalf, so I immediately drove to the courthouse and filed an arrest warrant for him. The clerk was shocked that I would file an arrest warrant on my own son. I told her why and finished by saying that his mother and I would rather our son be alive and in jail than dead.

There were times that we raised our anger with God and towards God. But we did see some God moments. It was these God moments that got us through, and if you have a faith in God, it is what will get you through your journey from grief to healing. Allow me to share three short encounters where God was already working for our healing.

The first encounter was the first time that my wife and I realized that we must include the police. Together we went to a police substation in our neighborhood to report stolen items. It was the start of the day, and for some unknown reason, the police were very busy. Soon an officer arrived and took our report and listened to our story. He was very attentive and caring. It was during our time of sharing what was going on with Matt that I saw them. On the officer's collar were two crosses that signified him as the chaplain. He confirmed that he was, but added, "I am also endorsed by the same denomination board that you are. My lanyard is on my dash." I was already dressed for work, and on the dashboard of his cruiser was the same lanyard I was wearing. Not only did God bring us a Christian officer, but a chaplain that was endorsed by the North American Mission Board of the Southern Baptist Convention. God was already there!

Encounter number two was on Thanksgiving Day. Matt was an inmate at the Kenton County Detention Center. My wife had been nagging me all morning to visit Matt, but I kept putting it off. When I finally did go, we struggled to have a conversation, not knowing what to say. As I returned to the parking lot, I recognized a man sitting in his truck. It was my adult Bible Study teacher. I had told him not to visit Matt because of the number of visitors Matt was allowed to have, but Gary had a bad habit of not listening to his voice messages. As Gary and I talked, we both realized that he was not meant to visit Matt. He was there to minister to me. If I had obeyed my wife's nagging earlier in the day to visit Matt, I would have missed Gary. If Gary had listened to his voice messages, he would have never come and never ministered to me. God was already there!

The third encounter occurred at the funeral of Matt's best friend, Kyle. Matt finished the program and had been sober for close to two years, but I knew that this funeral would be extremely hard on him, so I attended it to be a support. Once I arrived, I learned that the officiant was a close friend of mine in our hospice days. There are many fine funeral homes in that area, but the family chose that certain one and that certain one had on staff a personal friend that brought calming words for healing. God was already there!

In summary, I want to leave you with these important truths:

- Get educated about addiction

--Get support from family, friends, a support group such as Celebrate Recovery, Al-Anon, or church. You are not alone in this journey. That should be obvious by reading our memories of this journey from grief to healing.

--Do not give in to enabling.

--Above all, remain hopeful. After all, God is already there

- Paul

A Mother's View

After the loss of two babies through miscarriage, I asked God to give us a child. After eight long years, I became pregnant and had a son. We named him "Matthew," which means "gift from God." We had no idea the extent of the roller coaster ride we would eventually have with our son.

Matt was a happy child growing up. I was not working at the time, so we spent a lot of time together. We did so many fun things and had a great relationship. He was a good student, and the teacher always had good things to say about him. He was a preacher's kid, so a lot of times, life was not so easy for him. In his early teenage years, things began to change. He went from being happy, friendly, and a good student, to someone I hardly recognized. He became distant, secretive, and combative. He became extremely hard to get up for school in the mornings. Some mornings I just wanted to throw my hands up and just leave him in bed. We had such a great relationship up until this time, and it was very hard for me to understand the changes. I thought maybe these were normal changes in a child's life.

One day while cleaning Matt's room, I found a baggie under his bed with something that looked like dried flower leaves. I did not know what these were. I later found out that it was marijuana. I knew Matt smoked, but I realized now that he was smoking more than just cigarettes. I was upset and confronted him. To him, it seemed like no big deal.

Sometime after this, Matt had his wisdom teeth removed and was given Vicodin for pain. He ran out and wanted me to call and have the doctor prescribe more for his pain. I had never had my wisdom teeth out, so I did not know if the pain was that severe or not, but I did call the doctor and got more medication. Little did I know that this was the beginning of our lives almost being destroyed.

I still remember the day that Paul called me into Matt's bathroom and showed me needles that he had found in one of Matt's coat pockets. I was beyond devastated and just could not believe that our son was doing drugs. How? Why? When? He had a good family life with a Christian family. His father had been a pastor. How could God let this happen? I learned later that no one is immune, not even a pastor's family.

Things just got worse from there. On one of the times that Matt had been arrested, I asked the police officer if he could show me what cocaine and heroin looked like, as I had no idea. After he showed me, I asked him how much the baggie was worth. He told me, "$40." I was stunned. Every time Matt had a "problem" and needed money, he would ask for $40. I made the statement, "I have been so stupid." It was $40 to replace a window in his car that was broken. It was $40 for gas and cigarettes. It was $40 to replace a bad tire, and on and on it went. He would come to my office to ask me for money. All my coworkers kept telling me not to give it to him because they saw through him. I blamed myself for not seeing a pattern sooner, but everything he had asked for made sense, and being the "good" mom that I thought I was, I gave it to him. Eventually, this led us into bankruptcy. I wish I had been more informed about drugs and enabling.

My husband and I were constantly arguing with Matt and with each other. One time after Matt had been begging and begging for money, I finally threw my purse at him and just told him, "Here. Take it. Take it all." I think this was when I realized that I had to stop giving. I had no more to give... financially or emotionally. I felt like I was having a nervous breakdown. My son was an addict! I finally had to face it. I cried until I had no more tears. Also, during this time, my mother-in-law and my father died, my six-month-old grandson had open-heart surgery, and we filed for bankruptcy. How much more did God think we could handle? After all, He did promise he would not put more on us than we could handle.

Matt was in and out of jail, in and out of rehab, but the most difficult thing for me was when he seemed to drop off the face of the earth for about a month or two. He was running from everybody, and I knew there was a real possibility that he could be dead. I could not eat. I was a basket case at work. I was frustrated with everything and everybody. I learned how to be numb but continue going through the daily activities that had to be done. I learned to live with little sleep. Living this roller coaster was almost too much for me. I just wanted to drive my car into a semi-truck to stop the pain.

One day when we met with a police officer for guidance. She asked me if I had ever heard of Casey's Law. She went on to explain that this is when a parent, relative, or friend goes to court to have their loved one picked up by police and court-ordered by a judge to go to rehab when a bed is available. In the meantime, he would be in jail. Since an addict thinks of nothing but where the next fix is coming from, they do not realize anything else. They are incapable of helping themselves. This is a tool to get them the help they need. We decided that this is the step that we must make. People ask how we could have had our own son arrested. It became a choice, get him help or watch him die. So, we filed Casey's Law. It was not easy by any means, but if Matt was in jail or rehab, at least we would know where he was.

Visiting him in jail was extremely difficult. For a while, he was mad at us for filing Casey's law. But as we watched Matt slowly come off the drugs and become more "normal," we saw that God was working through all of this. He had given us an officer that told us about Casey's Law. A client at my work told me about Al-Anon and the chapter that she was the leader for. I learned by attending

Al-Anon that Matt choosing to do drugs was not my fault... something I desperately needed to hear.

Matt continued to get better and better. Was I afraid that he would relapse again? Yes, but I also believed that since God spared his life, He had bigger plans for him. To see Matt now in his dress clothes for work and helping others deal with addiction, we are truly amazed. We have forgiven Matt for everything he has done in the past because addiction is a disease. The addict cannot help himself. He is a living example that it is possible to become sober and stay sober. He truly is a "gift from God."

– Cheryl

Final Thoughts

I have lived the life of one of the most low-life, ruthless, and hopeless heroin addicts that you may ever hear from. My childhood was great. I was raised in a great home with great parents and great influences. Looking at the way that I grew up, you never would have thought that I would have ended up the way that I did. This goes to show that addiction can happen to anyone, regardless of their profession or their upbringing. It is just as possible for you to become an addict as anyone else. It is a scary thing to think about.

Addiction is killing our children, parents, brothers, and sisters in record numbers. This must end! Far too long have we been caught up in the argument of, "Is it a disease?" Far too long have we been saying, "They made their choice. Just let them die." Let me ask you, does it really matter if it is a disease or not? Who cares!? It is a major problem nonetheless, and people are dying. I should be dead, but I am not. I am alive to tell the world that there is a life after addiction. Not only life, but a happy life. Marriage, college, employment, children. No more worrying about going to jail if you have a court appearance. No more stress when you look into your rear-view mirror and see a police officer behind you. I have seen the worst of Cincinnati. Now, I can go to that city and actually see beauty. And wow, I never realized how gorgeous trees are!

No matter how hopeless, it is possible to break the chains of addiction. I am and will continue to be the example of the scum of the earth that nobody wants around if that is what is needed. I am one of those people who made their choice. I am one of those people that the world should have just let die, and I am alright with that. I am alright with that because I am here now to prove all those people wrong who feel that way. I will fight, tooth and nail, day and night, to change the minds of those people, for I might very well be the one person who saves their loved one's life one day. I will be the example of scum if that is what you need me to be. But, I will also be the model of hope for many others. This is why God kept me alive. Addiction is a very misunderstood and controversial topic. But, it is real, and it will not get any better unless we stop condemning addicts. We must get rid of the stigma behind the word and realize that we are people. The "real us" are simply hidden away inside of ourselves. We still love, we still care, we still have potential. We just need help. Condemning us to death is not a solution to the issue. There will always be another addict to take our place.

Throughout my life, I have seen both sides of the coin. Not only have I lived my life as an addict, but I have also had to be the one to worry about and bury my own loved ones. Kyle was my best friend. He was not my real brother, and he most certainly was not my child. But I will tell you that the pain that I feel from his passing is brutal. I cannot imagine what his parents feel. Through his passing, I have made a promise to never put another addict on hold. I learned a very painful lesson. One that I do not wish on anybody. Living drug-free is an amazing feeling and a great accomplishment, but it is not always easy, for I still must live with the guilt from that night. I must live and be okay with the fact that not everyone will make it out of their addiction alive. I must be okay with knowing that some of my friends will die because of it.

I have done my best to tell my story to the best of my ability. Please understand that this is my story and my experience. You may not share my view of certain topics that I have covered. That is okay because recovery is different for everybody. Do not get discouraged if you or your loved one does not remain sober after their first or second attempt at treatment. Keep trying! Love, support, understanding, open communication, and patience are crucial for everyone involved!

I want to stress to you the importance of creating good habits and practicing self-care. That could be getting a gym membership, continuing your education, or simply making your bed in the morning. No matter how big or small it may seem, they can all play a significant role in the recovery process. Routine can literally be a lifesaver.

There are many, many options for treatment and help for us addicts. I am only one resource. I am a very small, microscopic piece in the world of recovery. Help is everywhere. All you have to do is reach out for a hand, and someone will catch you.

Printed in Great Britain
by Amazon